AF598785

NAVAL

Fubuki-Class Destroyers

In the Imperial Japanese Navy during World War II

HANS LENGERER & LARS AHLBERG

Library of Congress Control Number: 2020952779

Designed by Justin Watkinson
Type set in Impact/Minion Pro/Univers LT Std

ISBN: 978-0-7643-6287-3
Printed in India

Published by Schiffer Publishing, Ltd.
4880 Lower Valley Road
Atglen, PA 19310
Phone: (610) 593-1777; Fax: (610) 593-2002
E-mail: Info@schifferbooks.com
www.schifferbooks.com

Acknowledgments

The destroyers of the Fubuki class were the first of a type that are sometimes referred to as "super destroyers," destroyers that were extremely large and heavily armed with guns and torpedoes and, of course, costly to build and costly to run. Other examples of early "super destroyers" are the Italian "Navigatori" class and the French Le Fantasque class, built in the 1920s. With the Fubuki class the Imperial Japanese Navy (IJN) took the lead in destroyer design, and the background is to be found in the Washington Treaty, which "forced" the IJN to expand the types that were outside the stipulations. Particular emphasis was placed on ships that were important for the night battle preceding the "decisive battle." Thereby the stage was prepared for the Fubuki class, and it introduced a new standard of Japanese destroyers, a standard followed by almost all Japanese destroyers designed afterward.

In compiling this brief history of the Fubuki-class destroyers, we are indebted to the following individuals who over a long period of time have given invaluable help in our research of the IJN: Messrs. Endō Akira, Fujita Takashi, Hayashi Yoshikazu, Ishibashi Takao, Itani Jirō, Iwasaki Yutaka, Izumi Kōzō, Kamakura Takumi, Kimata Jirō, Kitagawa Ken'ichi, Kitamura Kunio, Koike Naohiko, Maejima Hajime, Mizutani Kiyotaka, Morino Tetsuo, Naitō Hatsuho (via Itani), NakagawaTsutomu, Takagi Hiroshi, Takahashi Shigeo, Takasu Kōichi, Tamura Toshio, Todaka Kazushige, Tsuda Fumio, and Tsukamoto Hideki.

All photos are from the authors' collections unless otherwise noted.

Contents

CHAPTER 1

Introduction and Summary

The Fubuki class represented a completely different and remarkably modernized type compared with its predecessor, the Mutsuki class, regarding ship shape and general arrangement, and the more powerful torpedo and gun armament was in line with the principal torpedo operation policy and the policy of "individual superiority" over the American counterparts. Together with improvement of the habitability, in expectation of longer periods at sea, the ships were popular in the fleet, and their appearance was also noted by the world's naval powers. Before the appearance of this class, the destroyers from the Umikaze to Mutsuki classes were independently designed by Japanese naval architects, but their appearance, structure, and fittings resembled, more or less closely, the British style. In contrast, although also an independent design, the Fubuki class incorporated properties there were of "pure Japanese style," and it is no exaggeration to state that they determined the fashion of the succeeding destroyer classes and also of the "modern torpedo boats"[1] of the IJN.

The requirements of the Naval General Staff needed a considerably larger ship type, but from the viewpoint of the torpedo battle, light and small ships were preferable. In addition, budget restrictions had to be considered. The designers were thus forced to pack superior properties into a small ship. This task proved to be of extreme difficulty that could not be overcome only by conventional steps. Therefore, the Naval General Staff resorted to partly drastic means to reduce the weight of the hull, and they demanded the same from the engine and weapon designers. But these designers were not as successful as the naval architects designing the hull, and it was particularly the engine section that drastically exceeded the planned weight. Because of the pressure to keep the dimensions of even structural material as small as possible, the designers used very small margins in their strength and stability calculations, and these margins were totally consumed by the excess weight. On the other hand, and quite ironically, it was the excessive weight of the propulsion plant that compensated the surplus weight of the weapons mounted in the upper part, and made an immediate reconstruction after completion unnecessary.

In concert with modifications introduced in the course of the construction, which not only resulted in the usual division into three groups but brought about further weight increases, the ships were already in an excessive condition as far as these conditions (strength and stability) were concerned. But they had an excellent reputation in reference to every function, and few tacticians criticized them substantially.

The investigation after the "*Tomozuru* accident" in 1934, six years after the completion of the first ships, disclosed that the stability was on a low standard, and the "Fourth Fleet accident" the following year proved that the numerical and dimensional reduction of the structural material, in concert with excessive weight, had crossed the line when the forecastle had separated forward of the bridge of two Fubuki-class destroyers in a typhoon of hitherto unrecorded force. As in the case of the "*Tomozuru* accident," an investigation committee also discovered defects in the basic design process, defects that, for example, resulted in a revision of the strength calculation formula.

Every ship was improved by reinforcing the deck-plating and side-plating areas.[2] The stress was considerably lowered and sufficient hull strength was regained. In order to correct the raising of the CG (center of gravity), the earlier ships took on ballast, and those built after *Amagiri* received a heavy ballast keel. In this way, strength and stability again became good—without armament reduction—but the displacement increased and speed was unavoidably reduced.

The features may be summarized as (1) an improvement in seaworthiness (wave-cutting ability and resistance against waves, use of built-up large bilge keels to reduce rolling, arrangement and shape of the ventilation cowls of the engine and boiler rooms), (2) a closed bridge structure (the first attempt in a destroyer class), (3) a remarkable reinforcement of the torpedo weapons, including a reloading system (in fact, the strongest torpedo power), (4) the adoption of a slightly larger gun caliber and improvement of handling in rough seas (gunhouses, ammunition hoists, fire control system), (5) an improved habitability (living spaces rearranged, more and better fittings), (6) the adoption of cruising turbines (the first attempt for a destroyer propulsion system), and (7) the change from pole to tripod mast.

Miyuki sank accidentally on June 29, 1934 after a collision with her sister *Inazuma*. *Ushio* and *Hibiki* survived the war, but twenty-one ships were sunk by Allied aircraft, submarines, surface ships, and mines.

Special-type (*toku gata*) destroyers at the fleet anchorage in Ariake Bay at 1600 on April 6, 1939. This is a photo taken by Fukui Shizuo, and it shows the ships after having returned from a cruise to Aoshima (Qingdao). *Ships from the left*: the light cruiser *Naka* (flagship of the 2nd Destroyer Squadron); *Yūgiri*, *Asagiri*, and *Amagiri* (all of the 8th Destroyer Division); and *Ushio*, *Akebono*, and *Oboro* (all of the 7th Destroyer Division). *Kure Maritime Museum*

Hatsuyuki lost her bow during the 4th Fleet incident. The deck in front of the bridge was not able to withstand the stress generated when the bow was lifted by the irregular triangular waves. As a result, the ship lost its bow as far back as the bridge. This photo shows *Hatsuyuki* in Ōminato on September 29–30, 1935. *Kure Maritime Museum*

Storm damage to *Hatsuyuki* photographed at Ōminato on September 29–30, 1935. After the 4th Fleet incident, *Hatsuyuki* was towed by the heavy cruiser *Haguro* to Ōminato for investigation. The bow was severed, and it was later discovered drifting and was sunk by gunfire. As can be seen, *Hatsuyuki*'s bridge structure was also damaged.

Yūgiri lost her bow during the large maneuver on September 26, 1935. The ship was part of the 4th Destroyer Squadron (Dai 4 Suirai Sentai) when the force encountered a strong typhoon. At 1700, the bow was ripped off just in front of the bridge structure. Luckily, the bulkhead withstood the strain, and on the following day *Yūgiri* was towed to Ōminato by the light cruiser *Ōi*. On the right is the icebreaker *Ōdomari*. This photo shows the damaged destroyer in Ōminato in September 1935.

Fubuki undergoing modification at Mitsui Tama Shipyard in November 1936. After the 4th Fleet incident, the ship was docked and modified. The forward 12.7 cm mount has been removed so that the deck and hull sides can be strengthened. Note the rounded joint between the deck and the outer plating forward. *Kure Maritime Museum*

Another photo of *Fubuki* when under reconstruction. This is also an official photo taken by the shipyard, which was taken on the same date in November 1936. The after part of the hull is being modified, and not only gun mounts 2 and 3 have been removed but also the funnels. The modifications to the completed ships were extensive and were carried out soon after the 4th Fleet incident, and it was not possible for some naval arsenals and private shipyards to participate. *Kure Maritime Museum*

Amagiri during trials after modifications on March 25, 1936, off Tateyama. The bridge structure is lighter, mast and funnels are shorter, the voice pipes above the torpedo mounts are removed, and the hull is strengthened. At 2,340 tons, *Amagiri*'s speed dropped to 34 knots.

Miyuki arrives at Yokohama on September 5, 1931. The photo was taken by Fukaya Hajime, and all ships of the 2nd Destroyer Squadron visited Yokohama and then left for Yokosuka. Note the flare of the hull, not only forward but also of the sides. This was a result of the demand for destroyers with better seaworthiness. On June 29, 1934, *Miyuki* collided with *Inazuma* west of Cheju Island and was lost.

Inazuma at Sasebo on June 30, 1934, after colliding with *Miyuki* west of Cheju Island on June 29. *Inazuma*'s bow was severely damaged, and the ship had to be towed by *Shirayuki* and the light cruiser *Naka* to Sasebo. The lower part of the no. 1 main gun mount is crumpled, indicating the magnitude of the collision in which *Miyuki* was lost.

Along with *Hibiki*, of the third group, *Ushio* was the only special-type destroyer to survive the Pacific war. Here she lies disarmed at Yokosuka Naval Base on September 8, 1945. This is a view looking aft from the bridge. *Naval Historical Center*

CHAPTER 2
Requirement and Design

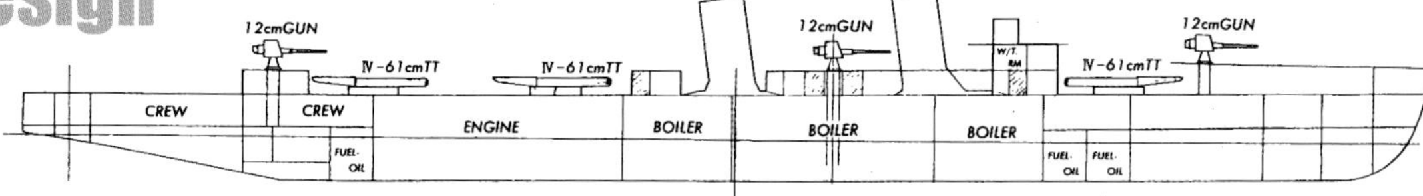

Outline of design F 41D. *Kansen Nōto*

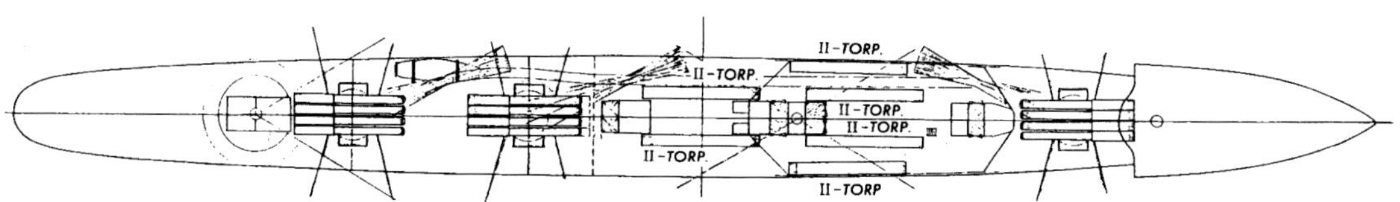

The Fubuki class represented a new type of destroyer, and the class differed radically from the preceding types, both in terms of properties and appearance. They were at first called "large destroyers" (*dai gata kuchikukan*, abbreviated *daiku*), but owing to their "epoch-making nature" this term was changed to "special type" (*tokkei*), and this is how the class is generally known. But why did IJN change the design philosophy of the destroyer so abruptly and so completely? In order to clarify this question, one has to go back to 1919, the year the Naval Education Department (Kaigun Kyōiku Honbu) submitted a memorandum about the future development of the destroyer, which promoted a tendency toward a heavily armed but compact type. The future destroyers should have (1) superior speed, by heavy oil firing only, (2) improved seaworthiness, to maintain speed in rough seas, and (3) reinforced armament, to be able to simultaneously fire six torpedo tubes in a day battle and nine tubes in a night battle, in order to improve attack and hitting chances.

In the following year the Naval General Staff specified its ideas of the frontline destroyers by requiring (1) the mounting of 61 cm torpedoes, with a 300 kg warhead and higher speed, as quickly as possible, and (2) increased speed and better seaworthiness.

Designs F 41C to F 41D3

Design number	Normal		Full load		
	Displacement (tons)	GM (m)	Displacement (tons)	GM (m)	Armament
F 41C	1,400	2.16	1.767	1.95	53 cm II TT × 2; 12 torpedoes; 12 cm I × 4; 32 mines; no. 2 minesweeping gear × 2
F 41D	1,430	2.12	1.767	1.90	61 cm III TT × 2; 12 torpedoes; 12 cm I LAG × 4; 32 mines; no. 2 minesweeping gear × 2
F 41D1	1.459	1.88	1.814	1.76	61 cm III TT × 4; 18 torpedoes; 12 cm I LAG × 3
F 41D2	1.469	1.79	1.826	1.69	61 cm III TT × 2; 18 torpedoes; 12 cm I LAG × 4
F 41D3	1.475	1.72	1.836	1.54	61 cm IV TT × 3; 24 torpedoes, 12 cm I LAG × 3

Source:
Makino Shigeru, *Makino Shigeru Kansen Nōto* ("Makino Shigeru's Notes about Warships") (Tokyo: Shuppan Kyōdō Sha, 1987), 145.

Notes:
1. This table reflects the condition as of December 1921.
2. The ammunition per gun was 100 rounds in normal condition and increased to 150 rounds in full-load condition.
3. The distribution of the three IV TTs of design F 41D3 is shown in the figure.
4. Designs F 41D1 to F 41D3 mounted neither mines nor minesweeping gear.
5. TT = torpedo tube; LAG = low-angle gun

In 1921, VAdm. Hiraga Yuzuru's "Study about the Successor of the Minekaze Class" contained draft designs of types armed with either four triple or three quadruple 61 cm torpedo tubes, thus not only increasing the diameter but also doubling their number.[1] Cmdr. Fujimoto Kikuo, who later became the main designer of the Fubuki class, also submitted a proposal about the same theme (December 8, 1921), but he gave his types so meager a torpedo armament that it did not respond to the trend of the time.

Particulars of Designs F 41E and F 41E1

Design number	Normal displacement (tons)	Lpp (m)	Armament
F 41E	1,530	102.11	61 cm III TT × 4, 18 torpedoes; one 14 cm I and one 14 cm II LAG
F 41E1	1,500	97.54	61 cm III TT × 4, 18 torpedoes; 14 cm I LAG × 2, 8 cm I HAG × 1

Source:
Makino Shigeru, *Makino Shigeru Kansen Nōto*, 148.

Notes:
1. 14 cm LAG = 100 rounds, 8 cm HAG = 250 rounds in normal condition (increased by 50% in full-load condition).
2. TT = torpedo tube; LAG = low-angle gun; HAG = high-angle gun

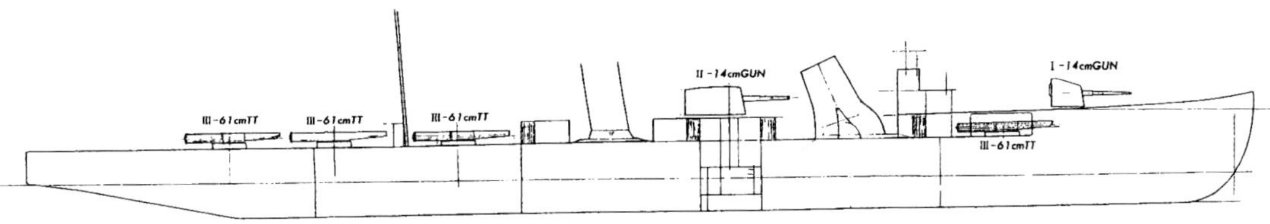

Outline of design F 41E. *Kansen Nōto*

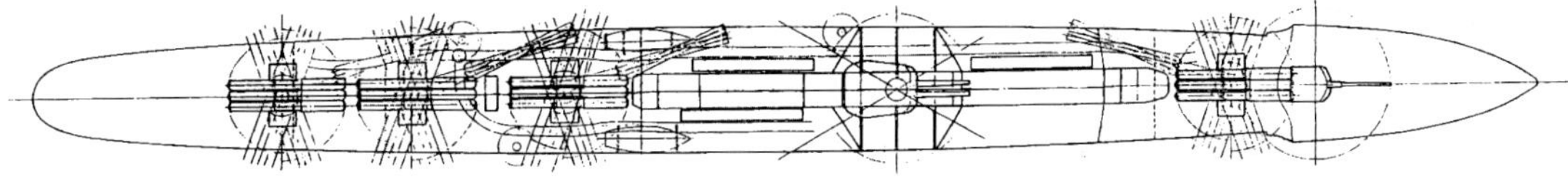

	Four Design Studies in December 1921									
	Case I		**Case II**		**Case III**		**Case IV**		**F 41C Kamikaze**	
Condition	Normal	Full load	Normal	Full load	Normal	Full load	Normal	Full load	Normal	Full load
Lpp	112.78		111.25		102.11		103.63		97.54	
Displacement	2,200	2.785	2,100	2.695	1,550	2,010	1,650	2.155	1,400	1,770
Shp	58,000		56,000		38,500		44,500		38,500	
Speed	38	34	38	34	36	32	37.25	33	37.25	33.5
Range	14–4,000		14–4,000		14–4,000		14–4,000		14–3,600	33.5–900
Complement									149	155
Torpedo tubes	61 cm III × 2; 12 torpedoes		61 cm II × 2, 8 torpedoes		61 cm II × 2, 8 torpedoes		61 cm II × 2, 8 torpedoes		53 cm III × 2	
Low-angle guns	12 cm G type × 4		12 cm G type × 4		12 cm G type × 4		12 cm G type × 4		12 cm G type × 4	
High-angle guns	8 cm HAG × 1		8 cm HAG × 1		—		—		—	
Machine guns	—		—		2		2		2	
Depth charges	DCT × 2, DC × 18		DCT × 2, DC × 18		—		—		—	
Mines	32		32		32		32		—	32
Paravanes	2		2		—		—		—	

Source:
Makino Shigeru, *Makino Shigeru Kansen Nōto*, 150.

Notes:
1. 100 rounds per gun in normal condition and 150 and 200 rounds for the 12 cm LAG and 8 cm HAG, respectively, in full-load condition.
2. Note that for each TT, two torpedoes were carried.
3. The original table is dated 8 December 1921.
4. G = gun; DCT = depth charge thrower

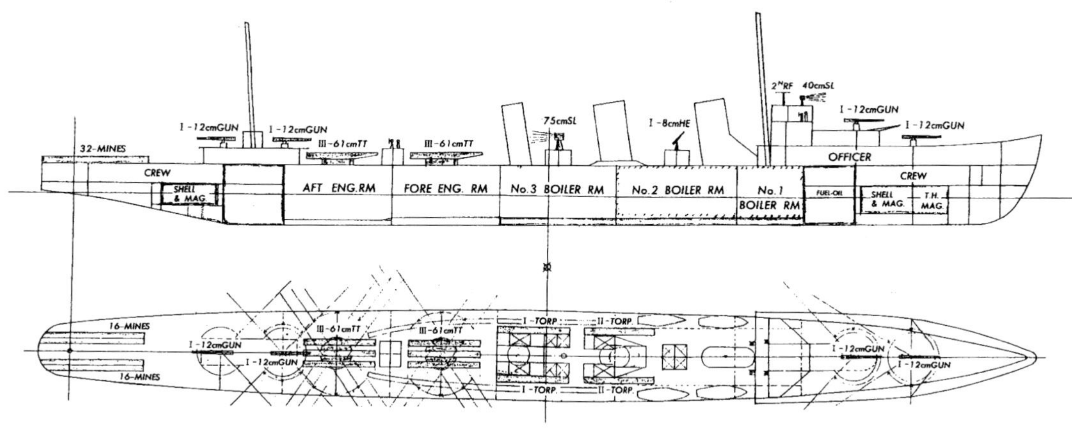

Outline of Hiraga Yuzuru's 2,200-ton type. The original is dated December 8, 1921. *Kansen Nōto*

When Fujimoto's proposal was received by the Navy Ministry, the representatives of the Japanese government were already negotiating the arms reduction at Washington. The treaty restricted the possession of capital ships (battleships, battle cruisers, and aircraft carriers) of the three largest naval powers, the United States, Britain, and Japan, in the ratio 5:5:3, and only two of the planned sixteen new capital ships, intended to form the backbone of the IJN's fighting power, of Japan's ambitious "Eight-Eight Fleet Program" were completed. The fundamental strategic and tactical conceptions against the primary hypothetical enemy, the US Navy, which were based on the battleship as the center of the fleet, had to be reinvestigated by the IJN because of the Diet's acceptance of the Washington Arms Limitation Treaty. Strategically, a compensation for inferiority was to be made by building auxiliaries with superior individual properties, and the decisive gun battle could then be fought on equal or nearly equal terms. In other words, about 40% of the US capital ships were to be sunk or heavily damaged while advancing across the Pacific. To attain this goal the IJN worked out the "interception-attrition operations" (*yūgeki zengen sakusen*) and relied mainly on torpedo warfare conducted by destroyers and submarines.[2] In accordance with this principle, the IJN adopted the following building policy:

- construction of heavily armed and seaworthy destroyers
- construction of long-range submarines with long operation period and particularly large torpedo capacity
- construction of high-speed, heavily gunned (20.3 cm), and heavily protected cruisers with torpedo armament, in order to break through the enemy's defensive ring and enable the destroyers to advance to the launching points

As for the destroyer, on October 10, 1922, representatives of the Naval General Staff, the Navy Ministry, the Combined Fleet, and the Naval Torpedo School, after having discussed several proposals, decided the following requirements for the most suitable type: (1) a concentration on torpedo attack, (2) a speed of 40 knots, (3) 61 cm torpedo tubes,[3] capable of launching more than six torpedoes simultaneously, (4) two twin 12 cm high-angle guns, but if enemy destroyers are armed with 12.7 cm guns, the same caliber should be used, provided that speed is not impaired, and (5) improved seaworthiness and hull strength, more powerful and reliable propelling machinery, small silhouette (i.e., a very compact ship). An alternative was also provided, and both are listed in columns 2 and 3 in the table.

But at that time, the Naval General Staff concentrated on a numerical increase of destroyers and postponed the construction of the 40-knotters because of the remarkable increase in the displacement, as expressed in a study of the Operation Division (OpDiv) of the Naval General Staff, dated October 16, 1922. On the other hand, the authors did not call into question that the new type of destroyers had to be realized in the next building program, even though with a somewhat reduced speed.

This study was forwarded to Dr. Hiraga on January 12, 1923, together with a letter from Cmdr. Kurokawa Kai of the OpDiv asking the Basic Design Section of the Navy Technical Department to investigate the details of future destroyers on the basis of the requirements listed in the letter (column 3 in the table). After a conference between the division chiefs of the Navy Technical Department, a committee was established. It was at first called the "Investigation committee of the large destroyer," but it was changed to the "Committee of the special-type destroyer" when, in outline, the fundamentally superior quality of the new type appeared.

The Basic Design Section was represented by Yamaguchi Tokujirō, because the utmost effort was required to be made to limit the weight of the hull without impairing its strength. The members worked out the requirements for a destroyer responding to the tactical conception of the Naval General Staff, using Fujimoto's previous rough designs as reference material.

The Naval General Staff submitted the New Warship Replenishment Program to the Navy Ministry on February 5, 1924, and the navy minister, Adm. Murakami Kakuichi, and the chief of the Naval General Staff, Adm. Yamashita Gentarō, conferred about the new armament program on April 18. The principle of the shipbuilding policy was the qualitative superiority of the individual ship compared to enemy counterparts, and Adm. Yamashita stressed that it had to be realized, particularly in case the destroyers had to fight against superior enemy forces. He stated that this feature required a large ship with heavy torpedo and artillery armament, high speed, and good seaworthiness. He continued by saying that thirty-six ships were necessary to compose the first front line of destroyer squadrons (desrons), composed of only this type. The concrete requirement is listed in column 4 of the table.[4]

During this time, VAdm. Hiraga, who had rejected a requirement of the Naval General Staff during the design of the heavy cruisers of the Myōkō class, had begun a visit to the United States and some European countries on November 22, 1923, to study warship construction. He returned on August 3, 1924, and his detailed reports about the large French and Italian destroyers and the tendencies in Great Britain and the US confirmed the correctness of the decision in favor of the "special-type destroyer."[5]

In the meantime, rough calculations had proved that a speed of 39 knots would require a displacement of more than 2,000 tons, and trial designs and reinspections were repeated. As a result, the Naval General Staff changed its requirements on February 25, 1925, as stated in column 4 in the table below. Compared with the former requirements, endurance and torpedo armament remained the same, artillery was slightly reduced, the displacement was dramatically reduced, and speed was decreased by only 1 knot.

Item/Date	I / 10 Oct. 1922	II / 10 Oct. 1922	12 Jan. 1923	18 Apr. 1924	24 Feb. 1925
Displacement				approx. 1,900 tons	1,650 tons
Armament	4 × 12 cm LAG, 1 × 8 cm HAG; 2 × III TT, 12 torpedoes	61 cm TT; capable of launching more than six torpedoes simultaneously; 2 × II 12 cm HAG (if the enemy uses 12.7 cm, increase to this caliber if speed is not lowered)	61 cm TT (six lines); 4 × 12 cm LAG; 1 × 8 cm HAG, 16 #1 mines; 2 DC throwers	3 × III 61 cm TT, 18 torpedoes; > 4 × 13 cm LAG (approx. 200 rounds per gun); 1 × 8 cm HAG (150 rounds); 1 × 75 cm and 1 × 45 cm SL; #1 mines; DC; paravane; hydrophone; wireless; 3 kW generator	3 × III 61 cm TT, 18 torpedoes; capable of launching nine torpedoes simultaneously; 3 × 50 cal., 13 cm twin LAG; 4 × 40 mm MG (or 1 × 8 cm HAG); others same as of 18 Apr. 1924
Speed	40 knots at 2/3 fuel condition in consideration of (1) reaching the releasing position safely and (2) escaping the blockade of enemy cruisers	40 knots (same reasons)	40 knots with 2/3 fuel (same reasons)	39 knots at 2/3 fuel condition	38 knots at 2/3 fuel condition
Range	Increase by 20%		4,000 nm	4,000 nm at 14 knots	4,000 nm at 14 knots
Purpose		Exclusively built for torpedo attack	Same	Same	Same
Notes	In order to attain 40 knots, a displacement of 2,000 to 2,400 tons was expected	Improved seaworthiness and hull strength, more-reliable machinery, small silhouette	Same Kurokawa's letter to Hiraga	Same; fuel storage sufficient for 5,000 nm has to be prepared	Same (slightly reduced characteristics but still too-heavy armament for the displacement)

Note:
It deserves attention that the insulation of the principal electric wires was particularly pointed out in the final requirement, in order to protect them from water and secure communication.

When compared with the Mutsuki class, then the IJN's most modern first-class destroyers, the features included (1) a remarkable increase of the armament (torpedo and artillery) by about 50%, (2) a slight speed increase, and (3) a very compact hull. What had begun with the heavy cruiser and had caused VAdm. Hiraga's job dismissal was continued with the destroyer, and the Fubuki class was the beginning of a series of ships designed with too many requirements within a small displacement under the premise of individual superiority.

Cmdr. Fujimoto Kikuo, who was the main responsible designer in the then Third (later again changed to the Fourth) Division of the Navy Technical Department, was in charge of the design of the future *tokkei*. He ordered his team to make utmost efforts to solve the contradictory requirements of "heavy armament, high speed, and small displacement." In the course of the design, new techniques were adopted and new ides implemented in order to attempt a reduction of weight. The hull, machinery, and armament were newly arranged and modernized. The design was made very carefully, and among the ideas to save weight, the reduction of frame dimensions, the expansion of frame space amidships, the skillful arrangement of longitudinal-strength members, the reduction of nonstrength scantlings, the abolishment of theoretically superfluous construction parts, and the reduction of hull plate thicknesses may be mentioned, while among the new ideas, the use of light alloys such as duralumin in the superstructure and the replacement of riveting by electric welding in several hull parts deserve attention. Everything was made to reduce the weight of the hull, but at that time, various relations were not completely understood and design techniques were not so progressed that considerable divergence from applied methods could not bring about unexpected results.

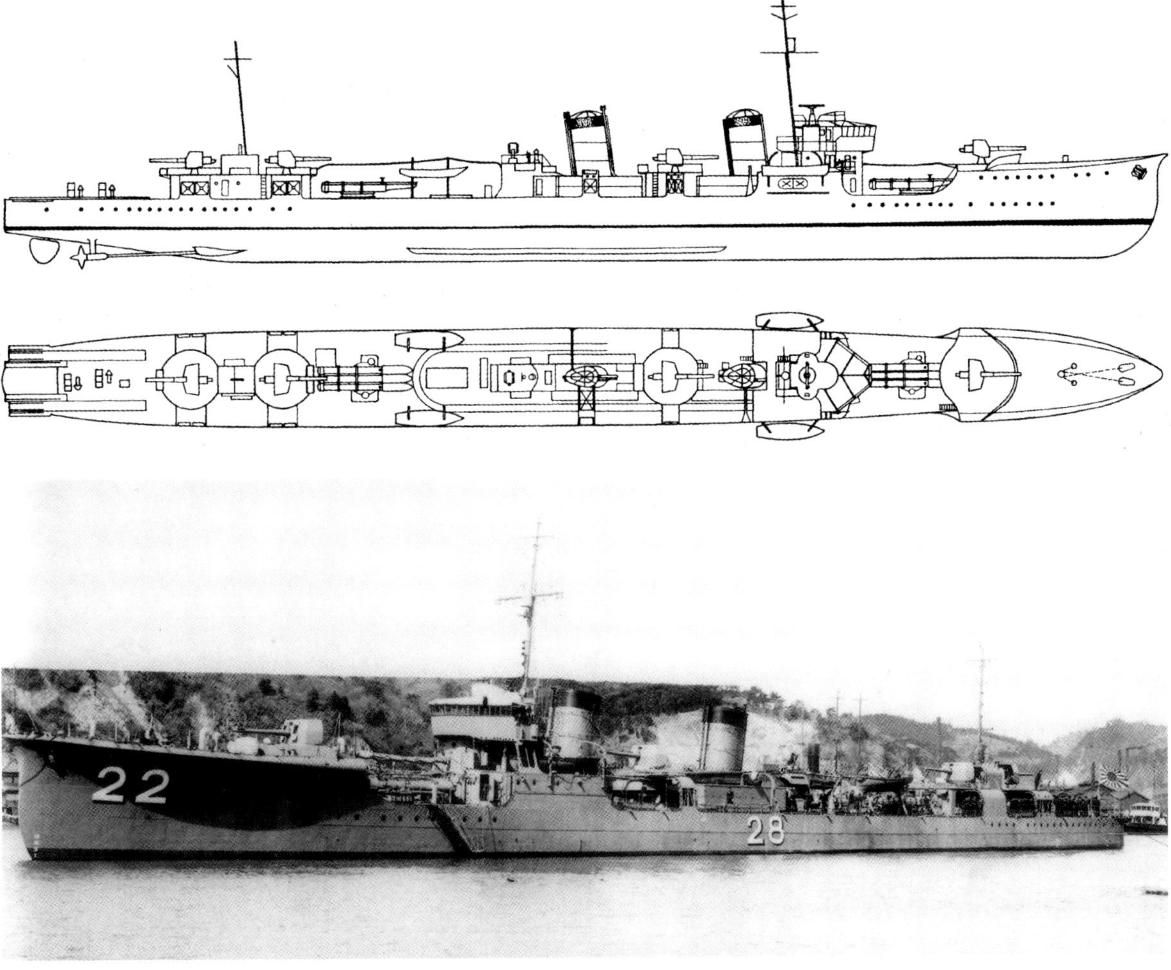

Mutsuki, the lead ship of her class, in 1926. This class preceded the Fubuki class. *Sekai no Kansen*

No. 28 destroyer, later *Minazuki*, of the Mutsuki class, at Uraga on May 22, 1927

CHAPTER 3

Construction

Between 1926 and 1930, a total of twenty-four ships were laid down, and they were completed from 1928 to 1933, as shown in the table.

Name and (former name)	Building yard	Laid down Launched Completed	Notes
Fubuki (II) (*#35*)	Maizuru Naval Yard (N.Y.)	19 Jun. 1926 15 Nov. 1927 10 Aug. 1928	1 Aug. 1928, renamed *Fubuki*; 1937, Shanghai landing operation; Hangzhou landing operation; 1941–42, WWII: southern advance, Midway, Solomon Island operations; sunk 11 Oct. 1942 by US cruisers and destroyers at Battle of Cape Esperance (09°06'S/159°38'E); stricken 15 Nov. 1942
Shirayuki (II) (*#36*)	Yokohama Dock	19 Mar. 1927 20 Mar. 1928 18 Dec. 1928	1937, Shanghai and Hangzhou landing operations; in-bay landing (northern French Indochina); 1941–43, WWII: southern advance, Midway, Solomon Islands, New Guinea; sunk in Dampier Strait while escorting Lae transport convoy 3 Mar. 1943 by bombs from US and Australian planes in the Battle of the Bismarck Sea (07°15'S/148°30'E); stricken 1 Apr. 1943
Hatsuyuki (II) (*#37*)	Maizuru N.Y.	12 Apr. 1927 29 Sep. 1928 30 Mar. 1929	26 Sep. 1935, lost fo'c'sle in a typhoon during maneuver off Sanriku (4th Fleet incident); 14 Jul. 1936, repairs completed in Maizuru N.Y.; 1937, China incident: Shanghai landing, Hangzhou Bay landing, northern French Indochina operation; 1941–43, WWII: southern advance, Midway, Solomon Islands, New Guinea; sunk 17 Jul. 1943 by US planes during transport operation to Buin (06°50'S/155°46'E); stricken 15 Oct. 1943
Miyuki (*#38*)	Uraga Dock	30 Apr. 1927 26 Jun. 1928 29 Jun. 1929	Sunk 29 Jun. 1934 after collision with sister *Inazuma* during maneuver (W of Cheju Island); stricken 15 Aug. 1934
Murakumo (II) (*#39*)	Fujinagata	25 Apr. 1927 27 Sep. 1928 10 May 1929	1940, China incident: operations off China's south coast and participation in the occupation of northern French Indochina; 1941–42, WWII: southern advance, Midway, Solomon Islands; sunk 12 Oct. 1942 after Battle of Cape Esperance. After rescuing survivors from sister *Fubuki*, damaged by US planes off New Georgia (Solomon Islands) and scuttled by sister *Shirayuki*; stricken 15 Nov. 1942.

Name and (former name)	Building yard	Laid down Launched Completed	Notes
Shinonome (II) (*#40*)	Sasebo N.Y.	12 Aug. 1926 26 Nov. 1927 25 Jul. 1928	1940, China incident: operations off China's south coast and participation in the occupation of northern French Indochina; 1941, WWII: sunk 17 Dec. 1941 by bombs from Dutch flying boat off Miri, Borneo (04°24'N/114°00'E); stricken 15 Jan. 1942
Usugumo (II) (*#41*)	Ishikawajima	21 Oct. 1926 26 Dec. 1927 26 Jul. 1928	1940, China incident: operations off southern China coast; 15 Aug. 1940, seriously damaged in Nanri Strait and repaired from Oct. 1940 to 30 Jul. 1942 at Kure and Maizuru N.Y.; 1942–44, WWII: northern area patrol and escort duties; sunk 7 Jul. 1944 while escorting a convoy, by USS *Skate* (SS-305) approx. 160 nm north of Etorofu (Kurile Island) (47°43'N/147°55'E); stricken 10 Sep. 1944
Shirakumo (II) (*#42*)	Fujinagata	27 Oct. 1926 27 Dec. 1927 28 Jul. 1928	24 Mar. 1936, performance improvement completed; 1940, China incident: operations off southern China coast and participation in the occupation of northern French Indochina; 1941–44, WWII: southern advance, Midway, Solomon Islands operations, patrol and escort duties in the northern area; while on escort duty to Uruppu Island (Kurile), torpedoed and sunk by USS *Tautog* (SS-199) SE of Kushiro port, Hokkaidō (42°18'N/145°11'E) on 16 Mar. 1944; stricken 31 Mar. 1944
Isonami (II) (*#43*)	Uraga Dock	18 Oct. 1926 24 Nov. 1927 30 Jun. 1928	1937, China incident: Shanghai and Hangzhou landing operations; 1940, participated in operations off southern China coast; 1941–43, WWII: southern advance, Midway, Solomon Islands, New Guinea, and escort operations; while on escort duty, torpedoed and sunk by USS *Tautog* (SS-199) in Buton Passage off southeast Celebes (05°26'S/123°04'E) on 9 Apr. 1943; stricken 1 Aug. 1943
Uranami (II) (*#44*)	Sasebo N.Y.	28 Apr. 1927 29 Nov. 1928 30 Jun. 1929	1937, China incident: Shanghai and Hangzhou landing operations; 1941–44, WWII: southern advance, Midway, Solomon Islands, New Guinea operations, escort and transport duties; 19 Dec. 1941, sank Dutch submarine *O-20* off Kota Bharu, Malaya, by shells and depth charges; when returning from transport duty to Ormoc, bombed and sunk by US carrier-based planes 70 nm NNE of Panay (11°50'N/123°00'E) on 26 Oct. 1944 (Battle of Leyte Gulf); stricken 10 Dec. 1944
Ayanami (II) (*#45*)	Fujinagata	20 Jan. 1928 5 Oct. 1929 30 Apr. 1930	1937, China incident: Shanghai and Hangzhou landing operations; 1941–42, WWII: southern advance, Midway and Solomon Islands operations; seriously damaged by US battleships and destroyers on 14 Nov. 1942 and sunk the following day 3 nm SE off Savo Island (09°10'S/159°52'E) (Third Battle of Guadalcanal); stricken 15 Dec. 1942
Shikinami (II)	Maizuru N.Y.	6 Jul. 1928 22 Jun. 1929 24 Dec. 1929	1937, China incident: Shanghai and Hangzhou landing operations; 1941–44, WWII: southern advance, Midway, Solomon Islands, New Guinea operations, escort and transport duties; while on escort duty, torpedoed and sunk by USS *Growler* (SS-215) 240 nm S of Hong Kong (18°25'N/114°30'E) on 12 Sep 1944; stricken 10 Oct. 1944
Asagiri (II)	Sasebo N.Y.	12 Dec. 1928 18 Nov. 1929 30 Jun. 1930	1932, Shanghai incident: Yangtze River operations; 1937–40, China incident: Shanghai and Hangzhou Bay landing operations and northern French Indochina occupation operation; 1941–42, WWII: southern advance, Midway and Solomon Islands operations; while on transport operation (Kawaguchi Force) to Guadalcanal, bombed and sunk by US planes off Santa Isabel, Solomon Islands, 28 Aug. 1942; stricken 1 Oct. 1942

Name and (former name)	Building yard	Laid down Launched Completed	Notes
Yūgiri (II)	Maizuru N.Y.	1 Apr. 1929 12 May 1930 3 Dec. 1930	1932, Shanghai incident: Yangtze River operations; 26 Sep. 1935, lost the fo'c'sle in a heavy typhoon during maneuver off Sanriku (4th Fleet incident); Aug. 1936, Maizuru N.Y. completed repair; 1937–40, China incident: Shanghai and Hangzhou landing operations and northern French Indochina occupation operation; 1941–43, WWII: southern advance, Midway and Solomon Islands operations; 16 May 1943, damaged by torpedo from USS *Grayback* (SS-208) NW of Kavieng (01°00'S/148°44'W); Aug. to Nov. 1943, repaired in Kure N.Y.; while on transport duty to Buka, sunk by gunfire of US destroyers (Battle of Cape St. George) on 25 Nov. 1943; stricken 15 Dec 1943
Amagiri	Ishikawajima	28 Nov. 1928 27 Feb. 1930 10 Nov. 1930	1932, Shanghai incident: Yangtze River operations; 1937–40, China incident: Shanghai and Hangzhou Bay landing and northern China operations and northern French Indochina occupation operation; 1941–44, WWII: southern advance, Midway and Solomon Islands operations, transport and escort operations; 2 Aug. 1943, rammed and sank USS *PT-108* W of Kolombangara Island; sunk by mine in Makassar Strait, S of Balikpapan (02°12'S/116°45'E) on 23 Apr. 1944; stricken 10 Jun. 1944
Sagiri	Uraga Dock	28 Mar. 1929 23 Dec. 1929 31 Jan. 1931	1937–40, China incident: Shanghai and Hangzhou Bay landing and northern China operations and northern French Indochina occupation operation; 1941, WWII: southern advance; torpedoed and sunk by Dutch submarine *K-16* off Kuching, Borneo (01°34'N/110°21'E) on 24 Dec. 1941 during antisubmarine warfare duty; stricken 15 Jan. 1942
Oboro (II)	Sasebo N.Y.	29 Nov. 1929 8 Nov. 1930 31 Oct. 1931	1932, Shanghai incident: Yangtze River operations; 1937, China incident: Shanghai and Hangzhou landing operations and power demonstration against France; 1941–42, WWII: southern advance, transport and escort duties; during transport to Kiska, bombed and sunk by USAAF B-26s approx. 20 nm NE of Sirius Point, Kiska, Aleutian (52°17'N/178°08'E) on 16 Oct. 1942; stricken 15 Nov. 1942
Akebono (II)	Fujinagata	25 Oct. 1929 7 Nov. 1930 1 Jul. 1931	1932, Shanghai incident: Yangtze River operations; 1937, China incident: Shanghai and Hangzhou landing operations and power demonstration against France; 1941–44, WWII: southern campaign, escort and transport duties, took part in the Battle of Leyte Gulf and was bombed and sunk by US carrier-based planes at Cavite Pier, Manila Bay (14°29'N /120°55'E) on 13 Nov. 1944; stricken 10 Jan. 1945
Sazanami (II)	Maizuru N.Y.	21 Feb. 1930 6 Jun. 1931 19 May 1932	1937, China incident: Shanghai and Hangzhou landing operations and power demonstration against France; 1941–44, WWII: southern advance, escort and transport duties; while escorting a convoy, torpedoed and sunk by USS *Albacore* (SS-218) ESE of Palau Island (05°30'N/141°34'E) on 14 Jan. 1944; stricken 10 Mar. 1944
Ushio (II)	Uraga Dock	24 Dec. 1929 17 Nov. 1930 14 Nov. 1931	1932, Shanghai incident: Yangtze River operations; 1937, China incident: Shanghai and Hangzhou landing operations and power demonstration against France; 1941–45, WWII: southern advance, Battle of Leyte Gulf, transport and escort duties; 3 Mar. 1942, sank USS *Perch* (SS-176) by depth charges (together with sister *Sazanami*) in the Java Sea; survived the war moored at Yokosuka in moderately damaged condition; stricken 15 Sep. 1945; 4 Aug. 1948, scrapping finished

Name and (former name)	Building yard	Laid down Launched Completed	Notes
Akatsuki (II)	Sasebo N.Y.	17 Feb. 1930 7 May 1932 30 Nov. 1932	1937, China incident: Shanghai and Hangzhou landing operations and power demonstration against France; 1941–42, WWII: southern advance and Solomon Islands operations; sunk by gunfire from US cruisers near Savo Isl (09°17′S/139°56′E) on 13 Nov. 1942 (Third Solomon Sea Battle); stricken 15 Dec. 1942
Hibiki (II)	Maizuru N.Y.	21 Feb. 1930 16 Jun. 1932 31 Mar. 1933	1932, Shanghai incident: Yangtze River operations; 1937, China incident: Shanghai and Hangzhou landing operations and power demonstration against France; 1941–45, WWII: southern advance, northern operations, Mariana Sea Battle and escort duties; 6 Sep. 1944, seriously damaged by torpedo released by USS *Hake* (SS-256) SW of Cape Bolinao, Luzon (16°19′N/119°44′E); repaired at Makō Repair Division and Yokosuka N.Y.; 29 Mar. 1945, damaged by mine near Himejima; used as antiaircraft defense ship in Niigata; stricken 5 Oct. 1945; 1 Dec. 1945, classified special transport and engaged in repatriation/demobilization service; 5 Jul. 1947, handed over to the Soviet Union as indemnity warship; 1963, scrapped
Ikazuchi (II)	Uraga Dock	7 Mar. 1930 22 Oct. 1931 15 Aug. 1932	1937, China incident: Shanghai and Hangzhou landing operations and power demonstration against France; 1941–44, WWII: southern advance, Solomon Islands and northern operations, escort and transport operations; during escort duty to Woleai Atoll, torpedoed and sunk by USS *Harder* (SS-257) 180 nm SSW of Guam (10°13′N/143°51′E) on 13 Apr. 1944; stricken 10 Jun. 1944
Inazuma (II)	Fujinagata	7 Mar. 1930 25 Feb. 1932 15 Nov. 1932	1937, China incident: Shanghai and Hangzhou landing operations and power demonstration against France; 1941–44, WWII: southern advance, Solomon Islands and northern operations, escort and transport operations; during escort duty to Balikpapan, torpedoed and sunk by USS *Bonefish* (SS-223) near Tawi Tawi, E of Borneo (05°03′N/119°36′E) on 14 May 1944; stricken 10 Jun. 1944

Note:
The budget for their construction was permitted in fiscal years 1923 (five ships, #35–#39), 1926 (four ships, #40–#43), and 1927 (15 ships). In accordance with the then-valid "naming" of destroyers, the first eleven ships were numbered #35 to #45, but because of the unpopularity of this system, names were given from 1 August 1928 onward, and so they became known as the Fubuki class.

After the completion of *Hibiki*, the construction of this type was canceled because the London Arms Limitation Treaty restricted the possession of destroyers displacing more than 1,500 tons standard. But this restriction had been forecasted, and after having enough ships to form two destroyer squadrons, the IJN stopped building this class, fearful of starting a naval race of large destroyers when the excellent properties of the *tokkei* class became known outside Japan.

The construction of these twenty-four ships went on over several years. During this time the technical progress was remarkable, particularly in the fields of weapon and machinery technologies. In order not to have retrogression, new developments were adopted as a matter of course, so that the ships were gradually modernized and improved. This process was in accordance with the building principle of individual superiority, something that was strongly required by the Naval General Staff. However, these modifications not only caused differences in appearance but increased the already serious defect of the weight difference between the designed and the completed weight. This means that the later the ships were built, the more extensive was the weight increase compared with the designed values. This had negative consequences on strength, stability, and speed.

The following tables provide an overview of principal particulars, coefficients and ratios, weight distribution, stability, and distinctive marks of the three groups.

Principal Particulars				
Item/condition	Designed (trial condition)	Completed (trial condition)	*Akatsuki* group	After refitting
Lpp (m)	111.99	112.07	112.06	112.0
Lwl (m)	115.31	115.75	115.78	115.97
Loa (m)	118.50	118.50	118.50	118.50
Bwl (m)	10.374	10.374	10.374	10.36
Depth (m)	6.25	6.25	6.25	6.25/6.268*
Draft, mean (m)	3.192	3.312	3.30	3.505/3.76*
Freeboard, forward (m)	6.628	6.488	6.50	?
Freeboard, midship (m)	3.057	2.938	2.95	2.745
Freeboard, aft (m)	3.138	3.083	3.05	?
Displacement, trial	1,980	2,096.6	2.086	2,270
full load	2,260			2,500.887
standard	1,680			
Speed & shp	38 × 50,000		38 × 50,000	35.45 × 50,000
Endurance	14 knots–4,150 nm	14 knots–4,800 nm		14 knots–5,000 nm
Fuel capacity	454	475		

Source:
Fukuda Keiji, *Gunkan Kihon Keikaku Shiryō* ("Outline of the fundamental design of warships") (Tokyo: Konnichi no Wadai-sha, 1989).

Notes:
* Means after *Uranami*
Average data; differences in various sources with regard to displacement, endurance, and fuel storage, but considered negligible for an overview

Coefficients and Ratios				
Item/condition	Designed (trial condition)	Completed (trial condition)	*Akatsuki* group	After refitting
Block coefficient	0.506	0.514	0.514	0.526
Prismatic coefficient	0.635	0.639	0.642	0.645
Amidships section coefficient	0.797	0.805	0.801	0.875
Waterline coefficient	0.763	0.766	0.765	0.769
Length/beam ratio	11.115	11.158	11.161	11.194
Draft/length ratio	0.0276	0.0288	0.0286	0.0302
Beam/draft ratio	3.250	3.132	3.144	2.956
Length/depth ratio	18.4	18.4	18.4	18.555
Depth/draft ratio	1.96	1.89	1.90	?
Wetted surface (m^2)	1.235	1.266	1.26	1.314

Source:
Fukuda, *Gunkan Kihon Keikaku Shiryō*.

Weight Distribution				
Item/condition	Design, completed	Newly built	After refitting	Design, newly built
Hull, total	**720.70**	**717.983**	**866.672**	**–2.72**
Hull	615.00	606.238	708.672	(–8.76)
Fittings	75.50	79.031	83.269	
Fixed equipment	30.20	32.717	34.397	
Ballast	—	—	40.234	
Consumable equipment	**16.32**	**19.701**	**18.456**	
Machinery	**685.00**	**805.590**	**804.733**	**+120.59**
Main engine, shaft, propeller	257.00	287.271	287.532	(+30)
Auxiliaries	48.00	42.453	42.503	
Boiler, uptakes, funnels	218.00	228.978	232.397	
Other (water, oil, etc.)	162.00	246.888	242.301	(+84.9)
Armament	**222.12**	**287.802**	**320.276**	**+65.68**
Guns	112.40	125.499	131.266	
Torpedo	77.80	119.237	140.911	(+41.44)
Navigation	1.70	1.594	(in torpedo)	
Electric	30.22	41.472	49.945	
Minesweeping, depth charges, etc.	(in torpedo)	(in torpedo)	8.154	
Crew, belongings, drinking water, etc.	**35.08**	**?**	**?**	
Other	**2.00***	**271.00****	**375.313**	** **official trial**
Heavy oil	—	243.00**	332.625	(not counted)
Reserve feed water		28.00**	42.688	(not counted)
Unknown	—	2.679	37.413	
Total	**1,680.72**	**2,141.100**	**2,469.339**	

Notes:
* Coal for stoves and other uses. In completed condition, 3.00 tons, i.e., +1 ton
** Not to be counted in a comparison between designed and completed weight, only the aforementioned 3 tons have to be counted. Therefore, 1,873.1 tons or an excess of 192.38 tons.

Before the shipyards received the drawings, very detailed weight calculations were executed in order to precisely know the total weight and to avoid the usual weight increases, but, as shown in the table, the increase was considerably more than in former ships.

The excess was particularly remarkable in the armament and machinery groups. An additional 65.68 tons or 29.7% in the former, and an additional 120.59 tons or 17.6% in the latter.

The hull and the fittings became 2.72 tons lighter than designed, and if the hull is considered separately, it became 8.76 tons lighter. This means that the weight of all other items was increased, and only the hull, upon which the strength of the ship depended, was built lighter than designed.

The total excess in weight was 192.38 tons or 11.45%. A total of 3%–5% more weight than designed was considered acceptable, without impairing stability and strength in ships designed with the usual reserve, but the Fubuki class was designed with almost no reserve!

The machinery, located near the bottom of the ship, had so much surplus weight that it almost compensated for the overweight of the armament in the upper regions. Therefore, the CG rose by only about 100 mm. GM decreased, but it had been calculated to be extraordinarily large at the design, and the ascent of the CG did not impair stability. OG was also reduced, but no serious problem appeared for that reason. The excessive weight of the machinery prevented the destroyers of the Fubuki class from becoming top-heavy ships after completion and saved them from immediate reconstruction. Ironically, the head of the Fifth Division of the Navy Technical Department was punished because of the excessive weight of the machinery (the result was a remarkable improvement of the design process and strict weight controls, and, in the case of the "*Tomozuru* accident," only the head of this division was not punished, and this may be considered another irony).

While the positions of the aforementioned weight groups prevented a significant worsening of the stability, no compensation could be expected in view of hull strength, because if the weight increases, the stress on the strength members increases, and BM (bending moment) becomes correspondingly larger. However, this problem was not recognized at the time and remained "hidden," but when the strength was checked, applying the then-worldwide-used strength calculation, no defect was found. The tacticians confirmed the excellent properties, and the ships had, as stated earlier, a good reputation. This may have given the impression that no limits had been exceeded, and since the design had been executed very precisely, the designers never thought of any "deadly" defect bringing about the "Fourth Fleet accident."[1]

Stability

Item/condition	Trial	Full load	Light load	Design (official trial)
Displacement	2,096.9	2,403.0	1,659.0	1,980
KG (m)	4.275	4.108	4.539	4.198
GM (m)	0.815	0.812	0.831	0.902
OG (m)	0.963	0.484	1.742	0.848
Range (°)				83.2
Wind pressure area / wetted surface				2.255

Source:
Makino Shigeru, Fukui Shizuo, et al., *Kaigun Zōsen Gijutsu Gaiyō* ("Outline of shipbuilding technique") (7 handwritten volumes, 1948–1954), 2:399.

Notes:
KG = distance between the keel and the center of gravity; GM = distance between the metacenter and the center of gravity; OG = distance of the center of gravity above the waterline; Range = range of stability

The wind pressure area was remarkably increased by the fitting of spray protection shields to the torpedo tubes and the large gunhouses. The long forecastle also contributed. But wind pressure area became only a design factor after the "*Tomozuru* accident," as was OG.

This table gives evidence of sufficiently stable ships, but this is true only for the earlier ships. If the third group is compared with the first one, the remarkable increase of weight and volume of the bridge, torpedo tubes, and also gun turrets can be recognized. This also contributed to the aforementioned increase in the wind pressure area.

These values represent the static stability. At that time, dynamic stability was not yet considered an important item.

Distinctive Features						
Group/item	Bridge	Funnels	Ventilation	Torpedo tubes	Low-angle guns	Machine guns
I *Fubuki* to *Isonami* (9 ships)	Small and simple without fire director and only a 2 m rangefinder atop	Two of the same height; top cut right-angled	Pipe shaped; vertically arranged abreast of funnel; curved 90° to aft; rectangular opening	No water spray protection shield (fitted later)	Model A; both guns mounted in a common carriage; 40° elevation; ammunition lifted manually; large, almost rectangular gunhouse	2 × 7.7 mm *Bi* type on platform forward of #2 funnel
I (a) *Uranami* (intermediate type) (1 ship)	Same	Top cut with bigger inclination	Mushroom type; circle-like arranged around the funnels	Same	Same	Same
II *Ayanami* to *Ushio* (10 ships)	Medium size with towerlike fire director atop and separate fire command station	Two of the same height; last four ships reduced height of #2 funnel to save top weight	Same	Same	Model B; independent movement of the guns; 75° elevation; ammunition lifted by hoists; dual-purpose gun but high-angle properties unsatisfactory; elegantly curved gunhouse	2 × 12.7 mm *Bi* type
III *Akatsuki* to *Hibiki* (4 ships)	Large with pyramidal-shape arrangement of torpedo command station, gun command station, and fire director tower. A 3 m rangefinder	One thin, round-shaped #1 funnel, one thick #2 funnel; only 3 instead of 4 boilers	Same	Fitted with water spray protection shields	Same	Same

On November 7, 1930, *Akebono* slid into the sea at Fujinagata Shipbuilding Yard in Osaka. The ship had been laid down on October 25, 1929, and was completed less than two years later, on July 1, 1931. No objects are visible on the hull, but it is a glorious moment for the builder and its employees. *The Maru Special*

Akatsuki is being launched at Sasebo Navy Yard on May 7, 1932. Note the large decorative ball (*kusudama*) at the bow. The hull under construction to the right is the destroyer *Hatsuharu* (temporary name *No. 59*), laid down in May 1931 as the first ship of the Hatsuharu class. *Kure Maritime Museum*

Hibiki was launched at the Maizuru Construction Department on June 16, 1932. The naming ceremony has been completed, and the gorgeous decorative ball (*kusudama*) has opened and released the doves and its confetti in five different colors. The ship is sliding gently into the sea. *Sekai no Kansen*

Fubuki with modified funnels on a photo from 1932. She was fitted with rainwater caps on top of the funnels from the end of 1929 until the spring of 1930. As a result, the forward ends of the funnels were raised and the caps were inclined sharply. This modification was carried out almost simultaneously on all type 1 ships up to *Isonami*.

Shirayuki at Kure on January 5, 1929, at the time of completion at Yokohama Dock (*senkyo*). Because of their large size and powerful armament, it is not unnatural that they were referred to as "special type" instead of the more conventional "Fubuki class" (*Fubuki gata*). The name *Shirayuki* is written in *katakana*, which is easy to read, on its side. Prior to March 13, 1915, names were written in *hiragana*.

Shirayuki about 1929. After World War I, the IJN began to prepare for battle against the United States, and since conventional destroyers were unsuited for operations in the Pacific, the IJN developed the "special type." They had high forecastles and prominent flare at the bows, and their seakeeping qualities even surpassed the light cruisers of the 5,500-ton type.

Hatsuyuki shortly after entering service on March 30, 1929. Immediately after completion, on April 3, the ship left port and joined the 2nd Fleet for training. *Hatsuyuki* became part of the 11th Destroyer Division, and the other ships in that division were *Fubuki* and *Shirayuki*. On June 29, *Miyuki* also became part of this division, thus forming a four-ship division. This photo was probably taken in Saiki Bay in June 1929. *Kure Maritime Museum*

Miyuki as completed. She was initially named *No. 38* destroyer, but on August 1, 1928, she was renamed *Miyuki*. The 11th Destroyer Division was at this time composed of four "snow" (*yuki*) ships.

Miyuki immediately after completion, photographed at an unknown location in late 1929 by Utsunomiya Shōten. The ship had been completed on June 29 at Uraga Dock (*senkyo*) and was immediately incorporated into the 11th Destroyer Division (Dai 11 Kuchikutai) for fleet training. *Kure Maritime Museum*

Murakumo in harbor in the Kyūshū area in early 1930, in a photo by Utsunomiya Shōten. She belongs to the 2nd Destroyer Squadron, with the light cruiser *Kinu* as flagship. The 2nd Destroyer Squadron consisted of only special-type destroyers and was a very powerful torpedo unit. On the after funnel, the ship has two white funnel bands showing that she is part of the 2nd Destroyer Squadron (after funnel), 2nd Unit (2 Bantai, two bands) (the 12th Destroyer Division). The 1st Unit was the 11th Division, and the 3rd Unit was the 19th Division.

No. 40 destroyer during a test run off Sasebo on May 15, 1928. Gun mounts and torpedo tubes are not yet installed, and no naval ensign is carried. The ship was completed on July 25, 1928, as *Dai 40 Gō kuchikukan,* but on August 1 she was renamed *Shinonome. Kure Maritime Museum*

Shinonome as completed in 1928. She was the sixth special-type ship. It appears as if she has not yet joined the fleet, and between the after funnel and the main mast can be seen the bridge tower of a Furutaka-class heavy cruiser.

Shinonome when part of the 12th Destroyer Division. She was built at Sasebo and was at first named *No. 40* destroyer but was renamed *Shinonome* on August 1, 1928.

Official Ishikawajima Shipbuilding (*zōsen*) photo of destroyer *No. 41* during trials in June–July 1928 off Tateyama. She was renamed *Usugumo* shortly afterward. Painting is not yet finished, but the 90 cm searchlight behind the second funnel and the 2-meter rangefinder on top of the bridge structure are already fitted.

Usugumo immediately after delivery, in a photo by Ishikawajima Shipbuilding, Tokyo. Her name is written in *katakana* on the side, but the spaces between the characters are too short and not in line with official stipulations. The name was probably painted by the shipyard immediately before the name change on August 1, 1928. *Usugumo* left Yokosuka soon after delivery and arrived at Kure on August 14.

Shirakumo departs from her berth in Saiki Bay in June–July 1929. This photo was taken by Utsunomiya Shōten between either June 16 and 20 or June 30 and July 9, when the 2nd Fleet exercised in Saiki Bay. At this time the 2nd Destroyer Squadron was gradually being reorganized with special-type destroyers in place of Mutsuki-class destroyers. The 11th and 12th Destroyer Divisions had special-type destroyers, and the 23rd Destroyer Division, *Mutsuki*-class destroyers. The ship beyond *Shirakumo* is *Fubuki*, of the 11th Division. *Kure Maritime Museum*

Isonami as built in Yokohama on December 2, 1928. She was completed at Uraga Dock as *No. 43* destroyer but was renamed *Isonami* on August 1, 1928. After completion, she was briefly used as gunnery training ship. In the distance is a Mutsuki-class destroyer of the 2nd Destroyer Squadron (23rd Destroyer Division). *Kure Maritime Museum*

Uranami at anchor in 1930. She belongs to the 19th Destroyer Division, together with the special-type I destroyers *Fubuki*, *Isonami*, and *Shikinami*. *Uranami* was slightly different and was referred to as type 1 modification (*I gata kai*). The ship had different ventilators around the funnels, and the funnels themselves had a different appearance, but she was equipped with the well-proven model A 12.7 cm gun. As can be seen by the three funnel bands on the after funnel, she is part of the 2nd Destroyer Squadron, 3rd Unit (19th Destroyer Division).

Ayanami on April 30, 1930, just after delivery, and this is a photograph taken by the Fujinagata Shipbuilding Yard (*zōsensho*) at Osaka. She is preparing to sail to her naval port, and she left Osaka soon thereafter and entered Kure on May 1. In the latter half of 1930, she participated in the fleet exercises. Note that the forward torpedo mount has a shield.

Shikinami at sea around 1930. *Shikinami* was the last of the "wave" (*nami*) destroyers of the special type, although *Ayanami* was completed later. Together with *Isonami*, *Uranami*, and *Ayanami*, she composed the 19th Destroyer Division of the 2nd Destroyer Squadron, with the light cruiser *Kinu* as flagship.

Asagiri departs Yokosuka on August 30, 1932. This is a photo by Hatakeyama Satarō, probably taken off Sarushima as the Combined Fleet (Rengō Kantai) headed toward Ise Bay via Tateyama. The fleet left Yokosuka after 1300 during a fine summer day. Note the 12.7 cm loading-exercise machine between the bridge and the no. 1 12.7 cm gun. *Kure Maritime Museum*

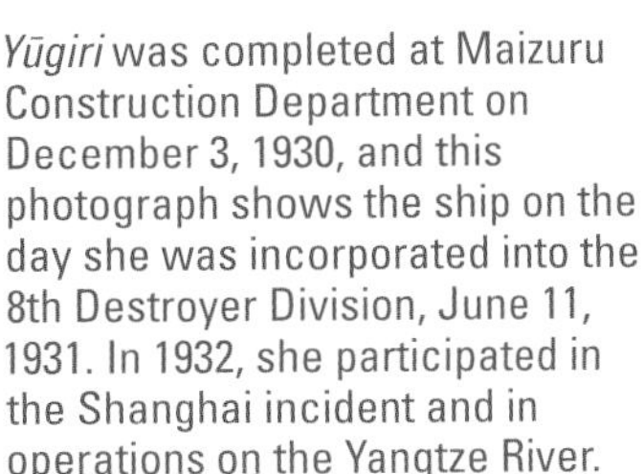
Yūgiri was completed at Maizuru Construction Department on December 3, 1930, and this photograph shows the ship on the day she was incorporated into the 8th Destroyer Division, June 11, 1931. In 1932, she participated in the Shanghai incident and in operations on the Yangtze River.

Amagiri at Tokyo Ishikawajima Shipbuilding Yard in November 1930. The second funnel appears to have been painted recently, and the bow draft can be read. It is written in meters every 200 mm, and in this photo the draft is 3.1–3.2 meters, which is very close to the planned draft. Note the rat guard on the rope to the left.

Sagiri photographed by Hatakeyama Satarō when leaving Yokosuka in September 1932. The ship had just been incorporated into the 10th Destroyer Division and is leaving for exercises. Note the white canvas on various places, including the 12.7 cm loading-exercise machine forward of the bridge structure. Not visible in this photo is *Sazanami* following in *Sagiri*'s wake.

Photo of *Sagiri* taken at about the same time in September 1932. The 12.7 cm loading-exercise machine, visible also in this photo, was used for training the gun loaders.

Oboro in 1932. After completion, *Oboro* was transferred to the 2nd Destroyer Squadron, 7th Destroyer Division, composed of late-second-group ships. The 2nd Destroyer Squadron consisted of the 7th, 8th, 11th, and 12th Divisions; this was probably the world's most powerful destroyer squadron. The torpedo tubes are unshielded in this photo.

Akebono was completed on July 1, 1931, and this photo shows her just after completion. No torpedo mount shields are yet fitted, and the 13 mm machine gun stand, forward of the second funnel, and the searchlight platform aft are uncovered. The ship is slightly inclined. Note the depth charges at the stern.

A photo by Hatakeyama Satarō of *Sazanami* departing Yokosuka in September 1932. At that time the 10th Destroyer Division was newly formed, and it underwent training in preparation for its transfer to the 2nd Destroyer Squadron the following year. In front of the bridge is a 12.7 cm loading-exercise machine. *Kure Maritime Museum*

Ushio photographed by Fukui Shizuo from the heavy cruiser *Maya* on August 12, 1933, when off Yokohama. Her crew is manning the rail during the rehearsal for the special large exercise of 1933.

Ushio at sea in November 1931. The geared turbines of the special type were capable of 50,000 shp, giving the ships a speed of 37 knots, but in books and journals the published speed was often as low as 34 knots (Fred T. Jane's *Jane's Fighting Ships, 1931* stated 35 knots). That source also said that the ships had nine 21-inch torpedo tubes.

The last four special-type destroyers used air preheaters in their boilers to improve their thermal efficiency. As a result, the forward funnel was slimmer and the funnel's inclination increased slightly. This resulted in a different exterior, so different so that the four ships became the third group (*III gata*). The first ship was appropriately named *Akatsuki* (dawn), and she was completed at Sasebo Navy Yard on November 30, 1932. This photo of *Akatsuki* shows her at Yokosuka in August 1933.

Hibiki as completed in April–May 1933, in a photo by Hatakeyama Satarō taken at Yokosuka. After completion, *Hibiki* was transferred to the Large Practice Force (Dai Enshū Butai), and it is presumed that the photo was taken at this time. As can be seen, the ship had shields on the torpedo tubes from the start. The cross-sectional area of the funnels was 1:2, but the narrow forward funnel had a circular cross section, while the after funnel was oval.

Ikazuchi in 1933. The background has been cleverly modified by the censor, and even part of no. 1 gun mount has been erased. After *Ikazuchi*'s completion (August 15, 1932), the 6th Destroyer Division was reorganized on November 15, 1932, to include *Ikazuchi*, *Inazuma*, and *Hibiki*. Around 1935, the three ships of the 6th Division temporarily, as a study, had their hulls painted olive for night battle.

Inazuma was completed at Fujinagata Shipbuilding Yard on November 15, 1932, and here she has been photographed, probably at Osaka, soon after delivery. She was incorporated into the 6th Destroyer Division, but as can be seen, the unit number has not yet been painted on the bow. Note the ship's very large bridge structure, and it is to be noted that the after funnel was much larger than the forward one, and their inclinations were different. *Kure Maritime Museum*

CHAPTER 4

General Arrangement

Because of the large number of illustrations, a description is thought unnecessary, and space will be better used for providing more data about the fundamental defects of this class. Therefore, only the features of this class will be outlined.

Seaworthiness

Among the many features, seaworthiness deserves particular attention, and it is well known from descriptions by the late naval architects Fukui Shizuo, Hori Motoyoshi, Makino Shigeru, et al. that the Fubuki class was better than that of the 5,500-ton-class light cruisers when these light cruisers operated in disturbed seas as flagships of a destroyer squadron. Makino's description of how a light cruiser was troubled by heavy yawing while the *tokkei* destroyer slid through the waves "in good shape," and was sometimes mistaken for the heavy cruiser *Furutaka*, is impressive to read. The reasons were (1) the adoption of a long forecastle instead of a "foxhole" in front of the bridge, and the location of the bridge at the after end, (2) a higher freeboard forward and a steep sheer at the bow, (3) a marked flare of the forecastle from the waterline to the deck, (4) an increase in the freeboard also amidships, and a smaller flare up to amidships, but aft of the bridge, the outer hull sides were curved inside close to the waterline in the typical "tumble-home" style.[1] The gradual increase of the beam from the waterline to the deck, like a flower in blossom,[2] promoted good wave-riding capability by its distribution of seawater to both sides and the immediate generation of larger buoyancy, which became bigger the deeper the bow dipped into the wave, until it was lifted up by the wave. It also contributed to the improvement of habitability by providing a larger space, thanks to increased beam (i.e., shift of the officers' quarters closer to the bridge), but, on the other hand, it caused more stress due to the raising buoyancy, particularly in case of rolling and pitching, and thus impaired the longitudinal hull strength.

Closed Bridge Structure and Shift of Officers' Living Quarters

Earlier, the open bridge had been considered a matter of course on destroyers, but people on the bridge were then exposed to rain, fog, snow, and other bad weather conditions, and sometimes they were also drenched by water splashes during high-speed navigation. This condition was evidently disadvantageous, particularly under battle conditions and long-time navigation. Therefore, from the viewpoints of navigability, habitability, and improvement of fighting capability, the structure was changed, and a completely closed type, with fixed roof and glass windows at the curved front and the sides of the compass bridge, was for the first time adopted in a destroyer class.

The height of the bridge structure was also increased by one deck, in consideration of the sheer at the bow and the mounting of the 12.7 cm turret a considerable distance forward of the bridge, which resulted in improved lookout and observation capabilities. In order to prevent vibrations, the continuity of the longitudinal and lateral walls was cared for, and much duralumin[3] was used in the upper part to avoid the heightening of the CG.

The private quarters for the commanding officer of a destroyer division and the commanding officer of the ship were placed on the upper deck, below the bridge. This was made in response to the demand that the commanding officer should be in a position to quickly engage, if necessary.[4] The officers' living quarters were also shifted from aft to the vicinity of the bridge. In this way, the big flare promoted the transfer and contributed to the improvement of fighting power and habitability.

Turret-Like Twin Main Guns and 61 cm Triple Torpedo Tubes

These were also novel features and are described in chapter 7, "Armament."

Height and Shape of the Ventilation Cowls

The height of the cowls of the ventilation trunks of the boiler rooms and engine rooms above the upper deck was increased and the shape improved, in order to prevent or reduce to a minimum the intrusion of saltwater splashes. The first group had them abreast of the fore funnel and fore and aft of the after one, but from the second group onward this arrangement was changed, and a mushroom-type cowl was put around each funnel. The latter type proved its value and also became a characteristic of the third-group ships. It also contributed to improved seaworthiness. It may be added that the cowls and ducts were made of duralumin, and it is said that corrosion by seawater was still more terrible than in the case of the bridge. The material was changed to pure aluminum, and its application was reduced.

Habitability

In concert with the substantial increase of the fighting power and the expansion of the operation area, an extension of the operation period was required. The designers responded with the improved habitability in order to maintain the efficiency of the crew. The crew's living quarters were made a little bit more spacious,[5] ventilation (motor-driven fans were used) and heating (a steam-heating system was introduced, and the coal stoves were used only when the ship was anchored) were improved, the galley was better equipped and fitted with steam heaters, and small (methyl chloride) coolers and refrigerators and a well-equipped medical room for stationary treatment were for the first time fitted in a destroyer. Storerooms were expanded. The sanitary fittings were also improved and, for example, one 10-ton-per-hour seawater pump was installed for sanitary use. Seawater and other pumps were generally motor-driven, and there were many more small details that were improved, which likewise contributed to improved habitability.

Tripod Foremast

The foremast was changed from the pole type to the tripod type, and it was made of steel pipes in order to lessen vibration and enable the abolishment of the shroud, which was often an obstacle. This type was used for the first time. The height of the crow's nest above the upper deck was 15.43 meters, and that of the truss was 19.68 meters. The aftermast remained a pole type, and its height was 13.20 meters.

Shipborne Boats

One 7.5-meter and one 6.5-meter diesel engine boat (*naikatei*), one 7-meter cutter, and one 6-meter traffic boat (*tsusen*) were carried to support transport of the naval landing force and to strengthen traffic and communication capacities.

Bilge Keel

The bilge keel was of the built-up type, instead of the past single-plate type, and the width was considerably increased to dampen rolling, but the designers were careful to give the ships a long period of roll—so important for weapon handling and the welfare of the crew.

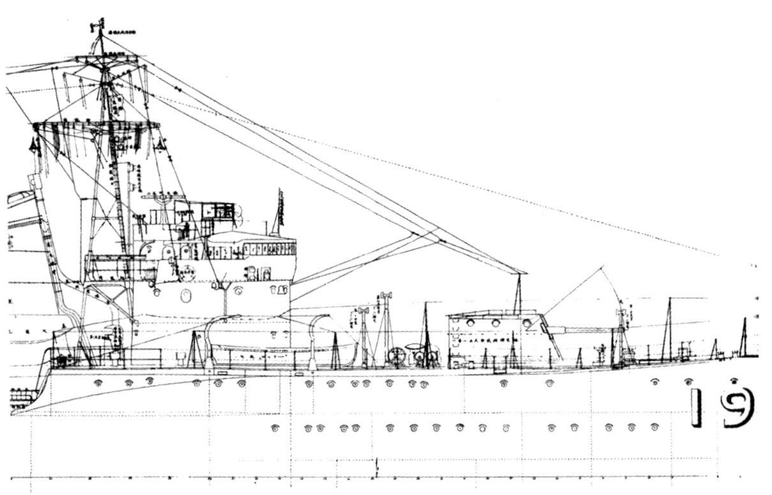

Bridge structure and no. 1 gun mount of *Uranami* after improvement.

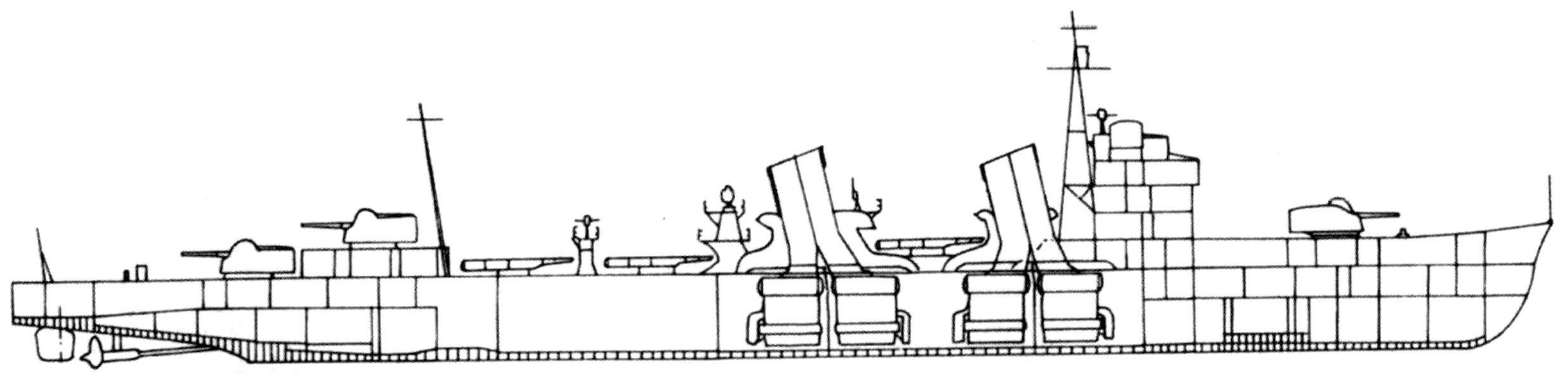
Interior profile of the Fubuki class. *Sekai no Kansen*

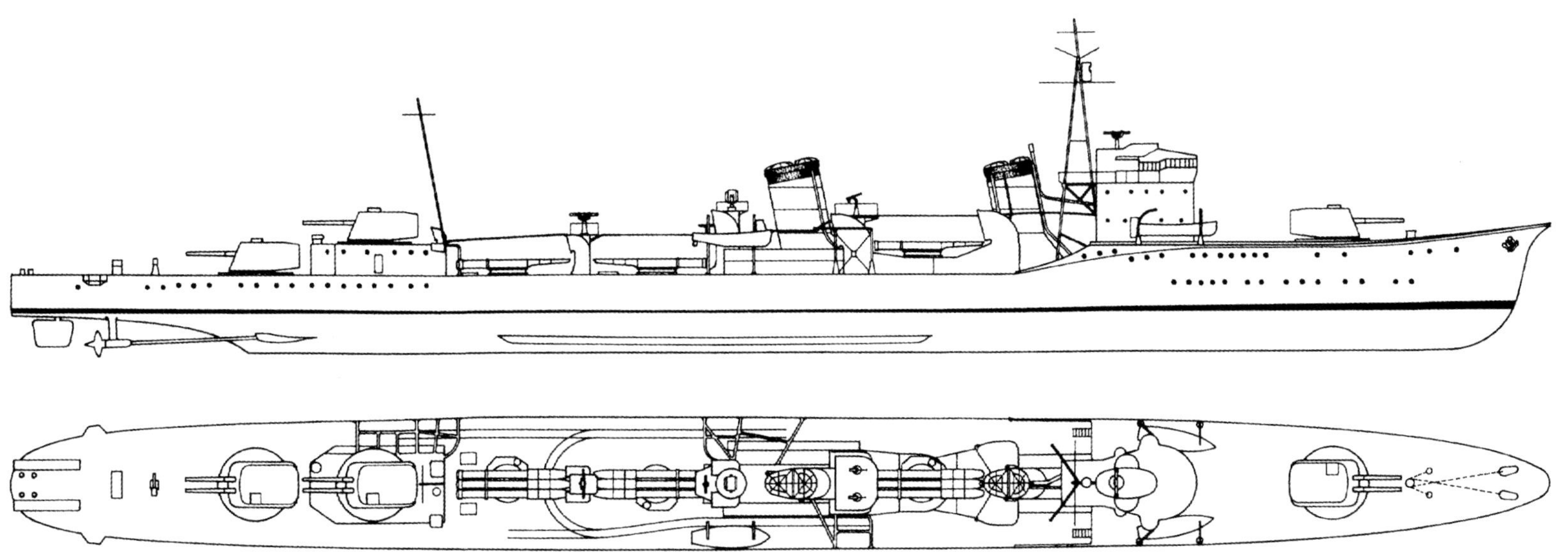
Fubuki as completed in 1928. She was a representative of modification I, with type A (+40°/–7°) gunhouses, unshielded type 12 triple modification I torpedo mounts, and large rear-facing boiler room inlets. *Sekai no Kansen*

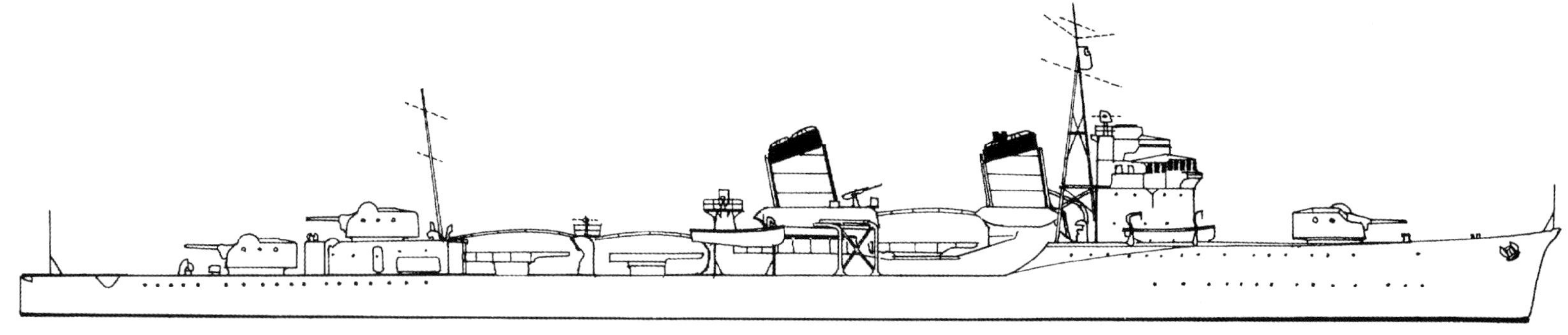

The modification II, with type B gunhouses (+75°/–7°), streamlined boiler room inlets, and a larger bridge structure. *Model Art*

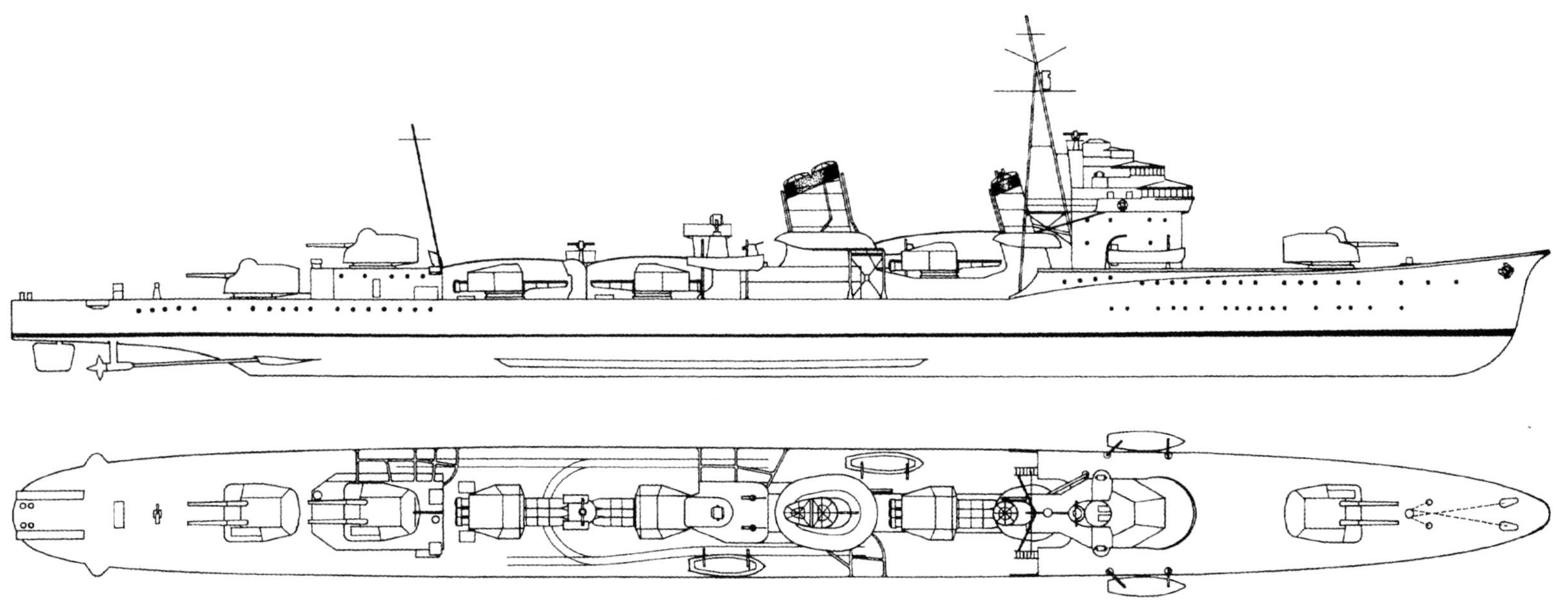

Akatsuki as completed in 1932. She was a representative of modification III, with type B gunhouses, shielded type 12 triple modification I torpedo mounts, a slim forward funnel, and a very large bridge structure. *Sekai no Kansen*

Fubuki leaving Tamano in March 1936, shortly after the modification. The 1936 fleet exercises had already begun, but the special-type destroyers undergoing modifications and belonging to the 2nd Destroyer Squadron could not join the fleet until April. *Kure Maritime Museum*

The 2nd Destroyer Squadron off Tokyo Bay on September 11, 1931. 19th Destroyer Division, *from left*: *Isonami*, *Ayanami*, *Shikinami*, and *Uranami*. 11th Destroyer Division, *from left*: *Hatsuyuki*, *Miyuki*, *Shirayuki*, and *Fubuki*.

Fubuki after modifications in March 1936. This photo was taken by Tamano, Mitsui & Company, Ltd., and she is probably leaving Tamano for Kure. The voice pipes above the torpedo mounts have been removed to decrease top weight, and the plating between the hull and deck forward are rounded to strengthen the bow section. Note the reinforcement frame on the 12.7 cm model A gunhouse.

Shirayuki enters Yokohama on September 5, 1931, and crew members are lined up to be prepared for mooring the ship. At the base of the funnels are large ventilators, much higher than conventional ones in order to prevent seawater from entering even in rough seas. Behind the stern of the ship is *Uranami*, a sister ship belonging to the 19th Destroyer Division.

Hatsuyuki at anchor on the Yangtze River on October 21, 1937. The photo was taken from the British light cruiser *Danae* during the early stages of the China incident. *Hatsuyuki* was transferred to the 4th Destroyer Squadron and participated in actions near Shanghai on October 20. Note that the ship is lacking a funnel marking. *Kure Maritime Museum*

Hatsuyuki at anchor in March 1929. Until August 1, 1928, she was called *No. 37* destroyer but was then renamed *Hatsuyuki*. With nine torpedo tubes, this was the most powerful torpedo broadside until the arrival of *Shimakaze*.

Hatsuyuki in Sukumo Bay on April 29, 1939. As a result of the *Tomozuru* and the 4th Fleet incidents, she has been modified. The funnels are slightly lowered to reduce top weight, and the voice pipes above the torpedo mounts are removed. The deck in the foreground belongs to *Akebono*, and the square structure is the rear end of the 12.7 cm mount (model B).

Miyuki around 1930. The IJN very much required destroyers with improved seakeeping capabilities, and the special-type destroyers were considered satisfactory. In size, this type was comparable to foreign flotilla leaders, and it set a pattern for future Japanese destroyer designs.

Murakumo in 1930. Initially *No. 39* destroyer, she was completed on May 10, 1929. The range of about 5,000 nautical miles at 14 knots was criticized by some as being too short.

Murakumo in about 1930. Compared with the first-class destroyers of the previous Mutsuki class, the special-type destroyers increased the actual displacement by only 25%, but the armament was increased by 76%, engines by 28% (engine power by 30%), and hull weight by just 20%. This meant that the weight of the hull was actually reduced, whereas a very powerful armament was realized.

Murakumo arriving at Yokohama on September 1, 1931. The picture was taken by Fukaya Hajime, and it is possible that *Murakumo* is about to depart to Yokosuka. The fleet then sailed via Ise Bay to Ariake Bay in preparation for minor exercises. The training year is coming to an end, and the ship is at its peak of efficiency. *Kure Maritime Museum*

In this photo of *Murakumo*, the censor has been at work, since the bow number ("12") has been erased. The photo is from around 1935. *Murakumo* took part in the operations off Malaya and in the Battle of Batavia (Sunda Strait), where the US heavy cruiser *Houston* and the Australian light cruiser *Perth* were sunk. *Murakumo* later participated in the operations in the Bay of Bengal and at Midway. She was lost on October 12, 1942, following the Battle of Cape Esperance. *The Maru Special*

Shinonome arriving to the harbor in 1930 or 1931. She belongs to the 2nd Destroyer Squadron, and at this time all twelve special-type destroyers belonged to this unit. The photo shows destroyers of the 11th, 12th, and 19th Destroyer Divisions. Behind *Shinonome*'s stern is *Hatsuyuki*, and beyond her, *Shirayuki*.

Shinonome in the autumn of 1932, after the funnels had been extended and the torpedo tubes had been fitted with shields. In December 1931, the IJN changed from four ships in a destroyer division to only three ships. Thereby, *Shinonome* was separated from the 12th Destroyer Division, and together with *Fubuki* (11th Division) and *Isonami* (19th Division), it formed the 20th Destroyer Division. One broad and one thin funnel band is a sign of the 4th Unit (20th Destroyer Division) of the 2nd Destroyer Squadron.

Shinonome on April 8, 1936. She has just undergone modifications at Kure following the *Tomozuru* and 4th Fleet incidents. This work had been completed on March 30, and this is a photo of *Shinonome* in Terashima Strait, by Hori Motoyoshi. The 1st Fleet had probably been on maneuvers in Ariake Bay, and it is estimated that the photo was taken from the heavy cruiser *Nachi*. To the right is *Isonami*, and beyond *Shinonome* is the light cruiser *Naka*, flagship of the 2nd Destroyer Squadron. *Shinonome* was lost on December 17, 1941, and thereby became the first special-type war loss. *Naval Historical Center*

Usugumo around 1931. The funnels have been modified and rain caps added. This is a good view of the model A gunhouse with its reinforcement frame.

Usugumo at Yokohama at 1100 on April 7, 1935. This was before the 4th Fleet incident, but some changes since delivery have already been made. The funnels have been heightened and torpedo mount shields have been fitted. Soon the ship will be included in the 4th Destroyer Squadron of the Red Fleet for the large fleet exercise in 1935. In the background is *Murakumo. Kure Maritime Museum*

A photo by Fukaya Hajime showing *Shirakumo* arriving at Yokohama on September 5, 1931. After fleet maneuvers the previous year, the funnels have received rain caps and their height has been increased. The shields of the gunhouses (model A) were very thin, and the ammunition supply was manual from below. However, it was a substantial improvement compared to the shields fitted on previous destroyer classes.

Shirakumo anchored in Osaka Bay between October 15 and 20, 1934, photographed by Furukawa Akira. The ship in the distance is probably the light cruiser *Sendai*, the flagship of the 1st Destroyer Squadron. The third-group special-type destroyers *Hibiki* and *Ikazuchi* are to the left and to the right, respectively. Both these ships belonged to the 6th Destroyer Division, and *Shirakumo* was part of the 12th. *Kure Maritime Museum*

A slightly modified *Shirakumo* with rain caps on her funnels. She was initially named *No. 42* destroyer but was renamed on August 1, 1928. The 12th Destroyer Division consisted of *Usugumo* (flag), *Shirakumo*, and *Murakumo*.

Isonami, which was incorporated into the 2nd Destroyer Squadron, in a picture by Utsunomiya Shōten in early 1930. This photo shows the ship shortly after taking part in fleet exercises. The first group of the special type ended with *Isonami* (the ninth ship).

Isonami off Sarushima Island when departing Yokosuka in September 1932, after the Combined Fleet had arrived at the base. The two white lines (one thick and one thin) on the second funnel show that the ship is the fourth unit of the 20th Destroyer Division of the 2nd Destroyer Squadron. Forward of this funnel are two single 13 mm machine guns, and behind it, a 90 cm searchlight. The tripod mast was made of steel tubes, but the mainmast was still wooden.

Uranami departs Yokohama for Yokosuka in early September 1931. This is part of a video photographed by Hatakeyama Satarō. The 19th and 11th Destroyer Divisions were departing in two columns, with *Uranami* in the starboard one and *Shirayuki* following (not shown).

Uranami departing Sukumo Bay in 1933. She belongs to the 19th Destroyer Division of the 2nd Destroyer Squadron. On December 19, 1941, she sank the Dutch submarine *O-20* off Kota Bharu, Malaya, by shells and depth charges, but on June 9 during the Midway operation, she collided with *Isonami* and had her speed reduced to 24 knots. *The Maru Special*

Ayanami departs Yokohama at 1000 on September 5, 1931. This is a well-known photo by Fukui Shizuo, and *Ayanami* is about to leave for Yokosuka after a five-day stay in Yokohama. Note the air being blown out from the crew's accommodation forward. At the stern, two rails for depth charges can be seen. *Shikinami* had left port only minutes earlier.

Ayanami at sea around 1932. The torpedo mounts are fitted with shields, but the voice pipes are still in place. The modification is still incomplete. The fleet exercises of 1932 were greatly delayed due to the Shanghai incident, and the long-term training at Saiki Bay, which was held annually, was not conducted.

Ayanami anchored at sea in 1932. The three model B gunhouses are trained to starboard.

Another builder's photo of *Shikinami* during trials off the coast of Miyazu. Although the date is uncertain, the sea state is an indication that the photo was probably taken on November 13, 1929. This photo well shows the superior wave-breaking properties of the special type. *Kure Maritime Museum*

Asagiri in the autumn of 1932. In this photo by Utsunomiya Shōten, the ship had a moment of rest before the minor exercise in the fall of that year. Two single 12 mm Vickers-type machine guns are mounted forward of the second funnel. Note the H-shaped funnel for the galley on top of the forward funnel. This was a unique feature of this particular "fog" (*kiri*) type of destroyer.

The newly completed *Asagiri* in 1930. Note the 12 mm machine guns fitted forward of the second funnel, the rather low position of the crow's nest on the foremast, and the high galley chimney (*hōsuishitsuyō entotsu*) on the first funnel, often used to identify individual ships.

Asagiri off Tateyama on March 29, 1936. She is undergoing trials after being modified as a result of the 4th Fleet incident. The deck edge forward is rounded, the voice pipes are removed, and the aiming room (*shōjunshitsu*) on the shoulder of the 12.7 cm guns is now flat. The ship carries a naval ensign, and the reason is probably that she is also performing gunnery tests.

On August 30, 1932, *Yūgiri* passed the island of Sarushima with the Combined Fleet. This photo can be compared with one taken of *Asagiri* at the same time. *Yūgiri*'s crow's nest on the foremast is placed above the yardarm, whereas *Asagiri*'s is placed over the yardarm. There are also differences in the arrangement of the steam pipes on the forward funnel.

After the 4th Fleet incident, *Yūgiri* was temporarily patched up at Ōminato and then proceeded to Maizuru for repair. She remained there until August 1936, when she reappeared with a strengthened hull and a newly constructed bow. This is a photo of *Yūgiri* (*left*) and *Asagiri* after modifications during an exercise in 1939. *The Maru Special*

Amagiri at sea around 1932. Twenty-four special-type destroyers had been completed by March 1933, and eight special-type destroyer divisions were assigned to the fleet. Four of these belonged to the 2nd Destroyer Squadron. A light cruiser led the destroyer squadron, and it was to make contact with the enemy fleet, and then, at night, the destroyers would attack with torpedoes, and with nine "lines" of torpedoes per destroyer, such an attack would probably have been effective.

Amagiri at anchor in 1939. The Sino-Japanese War broke out in 1937, and the number of foreign and Japanese warships in Chinese waters increased. *Amagiri* participated in the Shanghai operation and the Hangzhou Bay landing. At this time *Amagiri* belonged to the 2nd Destroyer Squadron, with the light cruiser *Naka* as flagship, and the 8th Destroyer Division, together with *Asagiri* and *Yūgiri*. *The Maru Special*

Sagiri at high speed off Tateyama on August 10, 1936. She has recently been modified, and this is probably a photo from the trials. The bridge structure is reshaped, masts and funnels are shorter, and the voice pipes above the torpedo mounts are removed, but the wires appear to still be there. As can be seen, her draft has increased and her speed has decreased to 34 knots.

Oboro during the rehearsal for the 1933 fleet review in Tokyo Bay. This photo was taken off Yokohama on August 24, 1933—a sunny and calm day—by Fukui Shizuo aboard the heavy cruiser *Maya*. Just beyond *Oboro*'s stem is part of the destroyer *Shiokaze*, and the destroyer behind and beyond *Oboro* is *Yakaze*. These older destroyers belonged to the *Minekaze* class. *Kure Maritime Museum*

Oboro after modification during the full-scale trial off Tateyama on July 22, 1936. The break at the end of the forecastle is changed, and the ship's overall appearance is more elegant. The torpedo mounts have shields, and the voice pipes are gone. *Oboro*'s speed was reduced, but this proved to be no handicap in actual battles.

A photo of *Oboro* from her companion *Akebono* while in Sukumo Bay on April 29, 1939. In the distance are the heavy cruisers *Kumano* and *Mikuma* of the 7th Cruiser Division. All of *Oboro*'s guns are trained to starboard, and laundry is being dried forward and aft. The ship probably has a day of relaxation between the intense fleet exercises. *The Maru Special*

The modified *Akebono* during trials off Tateyama on July 29, 1936. The hull has been strengthened, and the ship has received a heavy ballast keel. The voice pipes are removed, but wires above the torpedo mounts are still in place. Later this year she will be part of the 7th Destroyer Division of the 2nd Destroyer Squadron, with the light cruiser *Jintsū* as flagship. The 7th division consisted of *Akebono*, *Oboro*, and *Ushio*. *Kure Maritime Museum*

Akebono during fleet training in early 1939. This photo was taken by Matsudaira Nagayoshi from *Oboro* of the 7th Destroyer Division. Exact time and place are unknown, but it can be March 1939, when the Combined Fleet sailed toward Qingdao for exercises. The destroyer behind and beyond is *Ushio*. *Naval Historical Center*

Sazanami leaving Yokosuka in September 1932. In this view from the stern looking forward, it can be seen that the ventilators on the base of the funnels were placed quite high up. This was a "stormy weather" arrangement to make them secure from the inrush of water. On the stern is the name *Sazanami* written in white *hiragana* characters from right to left. *Kure Maritime Museum*

Sazanami at slow speed en route to Yokosuka in July 1932. She had been built at Maizuru and was completed on May 19, 1932, and was the last ship of the Fubuki class with four boilers. *Maruzen*

Ushio during trials on August 4, 1936, off Tateyama, after her "express" modification following the *Tomozuru* and 4th Fleet incidents. She was then incorporated into the 4th Torpedo Squadron of the Red Fleet during the exercises in 1936, and an identification band is painted on the forward funnel. The practice of applying funnel bands on the first funnel for the 1st Destroyer Squadron and on the second funnel for the 2nd Destroyer Squadron came into use in 1921 and was used until 1941.

Ushio during high-speed cruising about 1937. After modifications, *Ushio* returned to the 2nd Torpedo Squadron with *Oboro* and *Akebono*, as the 7th Destroyer Division. In 1940, together with *Akebono*, *Oboro*, and *Sazanami*, she was moved to the 7th Division of the 4th Torpedo Squadron. *The Maru Special*

Akatsuki during trials off Tateyama on January 18, 1937. She has been modified, and the remarkably large bridge structure that she had on completion has been reduced in size. In this group of special-type destroyers, the number of boilers was reduced from four to three, and this is the reason why the forward funnel is so narrow.

Hibiki at anchor off Yokosuka in 1933, with awnings spread. The beautiful flare of the forecastle is obvious in this view. Later the ship was transferred to the 2nd Destroyer Squadron, 6th Destroyer Division, at Yokosuka. This division consisted of *Inazuma*, *Ikazuchi*, and *Hibiki*. From this angle, the complicated bridge structure is clearly visible, and the structure almost resembled that of a heavy cruiser. However, this affected stability more than in the earlier ships.

Hibiki on the Yangtze River in the early days of the China incident, in a photo by the Royal Navy taken in early December 1937. The destroyer in the background, behind the no. 1 gun mount, is probably *Asashio* (completed in August 1937), lead ship of the Asashio class. So many changes since completion have been made to *Hibiki* that it almost appears to be a new ship. *Kure Maritime Museum*

Ikazuchi off the coast of Nagaura, Yokosuka, in 1933. The purpose of the large inclination of the forward funnel was to keep smoke away from the 3-meter rangefinder and the compass bridge. It was also rather low, so as not to obstruct the rear view. The boiler weight was reduced by 58 tons compared to the first and second groups of the special type, and it is said that fuel consumption decreased by 14%.

Ikazuchi after modification in Uraga Channel on April 11, 1936. This photo was taken as *Ikazuchi* was heading to Tateyama for speed trials. The official test result on that day was 2,466 tons, 51,114 shp, and 33.46 knots. The white bands on the second funnel indicate that the ship was being incorporated into the 2nd Destroyer Squadron. The text in the right corner merely says that this is a photo of the destroyer *Ikazuchi* on full-power trials after modification on April 11, 1936.

The modified *Inazuma* running trials off Maizuru on March 24, 1936. The upper part of the bridge structure is thoroughly remodeled. The trial displacement increased from 2,050 to 2,450 tons, but the speed dropped to 34.5 from 37.5 knots. However, stability and strength were substantially improved, and *Inazuma* became a very powerful destroyer.

Inazuma at sea in 1937. She had been modified and was still with the 6th Destroyer Division during the occupation of Hong Kong in December 1941. On January 20, 1942, she collided with the storeship *Sendai Maru* off Davao and was repaired at Mako, Pescadores. *Inazuma* then took part in the Aleutians and Solomons campaigns. She was sunk on May 14, 1944, by the US submarine *Bonefish* in the Celebes Sea, near Tawi Tawi. *The Maru Special*

Yūgiri's compass bridge in October 1941. This is a view from the center near the port side, looking forward. The cylindrical object slightly to the right is a magnetic compass. At the right end is the steering wheel, and forward of it the steering telemotor. Also visible are 12 cm binoculars. *Sekai no Kansen*

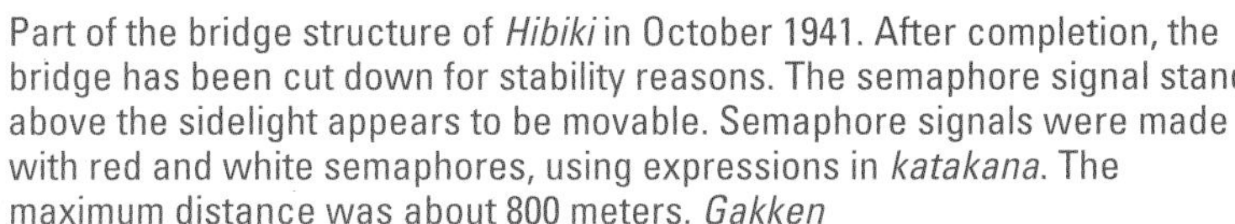

Part of the bridge structure of *Hibiki* in October 1941. After completion, the bridge has been cut down for stability reasons. The semaphore signal stand above the sidelight appears to be movable. Semaphore signals were made with red and white semaphores, using expressions in *katakana*. The maximum distance was about 800 meters. *Gakken*

The ladder for climbing up to the crow's nest on *Isonami*. The bow of the ship is to the right of the picture. On the right hand are two boxlike connected "string-type" recognition lights extending downward. The black area at the lower left is probably the stand for the 2 kW signal light, so the shooting time must be after 1940. *Gakken*

The midpart of *Oboro* in 1939. This is a starboard view from the vicinity of the torpedo mount no. 2, behind the second funnel, looking forward. The large canvas-covered object is the 90 cm searchlight. It appears as if *Oboro* was lacking the loop antenna when this photo was taken. The 2-meter rangefinder on top of the bridge structure can be seen. Note the skid beams used for torpedo transport. *The Maru Special*

Akebono during fleet training in early 1939. The photo was taken by Matsudaira Nagayoshi aboard the leading ship *Oboro*. The destroyer in the wake of *Akebono* is *Ushio*. *Akebono* is in a high-speed course change with hard right rudder, and her after main guns are trained to starboard. *Kure Maritime Museum*

Part of the 8th Destroyer Division of the 2nd Destroyer Squadron on exercises off the coast of Kujūkuri, Chiba Prefecture, in 1939. *Asagiri* (*left*) and *Yūgiri* (*to the right*) are moving at high speed. The 8th Destroyer Division was composed of three ships, *Asagiri*, *Yūgiri*, and *Amagiri*, but in November they were transferred to Kure and became the 20th Destroyer Division. *The Maru Special*

Sazanami on April 15, 1940, after completing her modification at Uraga Dock. She had temporarily been withdrawn from the 7th Destroyer Division but was returned on the date of the photo. This picture was taken just before she set course for Yokosuka. No division numeral is shown, and forward of the second funnel is probably a twin 13 mm machine gun mount.

Usugumo (*right*) at anchor with *Shinonome* (*beyond*) in 1940. This photo was taken from *Murakumo*, of the same destroyer division. The one-funneled ships in the distance and to the left are torpedo boats. *Usugumo* was seriously damaged by a mine in Nanri Strait on August 15, 1940, and was under repair until July 30, 1942, at Kure and Maizuru. *The Maru Special*

Destroyers of the 20th Destroyer Division at sea during an exercise in October 1941. *Sagiri* is leading *Amagiri* (*left*) and *Asagiri* (*right*). The fourth ship (*Yūgiri*) is not shown. At this time, each destroyer squadron consisted of four destroyer divisions, and each division had four ships. It was expected, or hoped, that one enemy battleship could be torpedoed by one division (32–36 "lines") and that four enemy ships could be destroyed by a destroyer squadron. Signal flags displayed by *Sagiri* are, *from the top*, special classification flag, counting numbers (distance) (*Shingōkubetsuki* [*Kei*]), number flag (8) (*Sūjiki* [*8*]), and letter flag (P) (*Mojiki* [*P*]).

The 20th Destroyer Division on maneuvers in October 1941. *Sagiri* is followed by *Amagiri* and *Asagiri* in this photo taken from the lead ship, *Yūgiri*. Guns are trained to starboard, and the ships are moving at low speed to form a single column. All four destroyers of the division were of the second group of special-type destroyers, and at times these four were called the "fog group" (*kiri gurūpu*).

Hibiki at sea around December 10, 1941. The ship is receiving important documents from the heavy cruiser *Atago*, and a high line has been passed while the two ships are sailing parallel at 14–16 knots. This photo was probably taken before *Hibiki* entered Camranh Bay. A degaussing coil is attached to the hull, and the bridge structure has been reduced in size. *Hibiki*'s name and the number of the destroyer division both have been painted out, a practice used during the Pacific war. It is not known what the character *I* (い), written on the bridge, means, but it could mean the 1st Destroyer Squadron. If so, *Ro* (ろ) would mean the 2nd Destroyer Squadron.

Isonami in no. 4 dock at Yokosuka on June 16, 1942. While participating in the Midway operation (3rd Destroyer Squadron, 19th Destroyer Division), she collided with *Uranami* on June 9 and suffered a damaged bow, and her speed dropped to 11 knots. Although the plating below the waterline was smashed, repairs were completed in a short time, and by July 20 it was finished. Note the degaussing coil running along the upper edge of the hull. *Kure Maritime Museum*

A photo of *Ushio* at Ōminato in late April 1942. *Ushio* together with *Akebono* and *Sazanami* formed the 7th Destroyer Division, and they participated in the Aleutians operation along with the aircraft carriers *Ryūjō* and *Junyō*. The distant tanker is *Teiyō Maru*, and to the right is the stern of the transport *Kinugasa Maru*. *The Maru Special*

Hibiki in damaged condition at Ōminato on July 3, 1942. On June 12, *Hibiki* was at anchor of Kiska Island, when she was damaged by bombs during a surprise attack by US PBYs. Her bow was severely damaged and her speed was reduced. She returned to Ōminato for emergency repairs and then proceeded to Yokosuka to be docked and repaired. In this photo the damaged bow section has been removed. Note the stamp of "Secret" on the picture. *Kure Maritime Museum*

Hibiki off Kiska Island immediately after the air attack on June 12, 1942. The bow section is damaged by near misses, and there is a hole near the waterline almost below the no. 1 gun mount. Fortunately, it was possible to proceed to Ōminato for temporary repairs. *The Maru Special*

Akatsuki photographed off Kiska by Furukawa Akira during, probably, the Aleutians operation in June–August 1942. At this time the ship belonged to the 1st Destroyer Squadron and the white bands on the forward funnel indicate that she is the 4th unit. Funnel bands were used by the IJN almost throughout the Pacific war, and the last recorded use was on a Yūgumo-class destroyer at Ormoc Bay on November 14, 1944. It is not impossible that this photo of *Akatsuki* was taken in February–April 1943. *Naval Historical Center*

Probably *Fubuki* during operations in the vicinity of the Solomon Islands. The photo was taken from the heavy cruiser *Aoba* three days prior to the Battle of Cape Esperance (October 11, 1942). During the battle, *Fubuki* was heavily damaged amidships by shellfire and sank at 2212; 119 crew members survived the loss, with 111 rescued by US forces and eight by the Japanese. *The Maru Special*

Shirayuki proceeding at high speed during the Battle of the Bismarck Sea on March 3, 1943. *Shirayuki* was the flagship of a convoy bringing reinforcements from Rabaul to Lae when the convoy was attacked by Allied airplanes. The ship was lethally damaged by skip-bombing and went down 55 miles southeast of Finschafen. The convoy was lost, as were four of the eight escorting destroyers. *The Maru Special*

During a storm on March 30, 1943, *Ikazuchi* collided with the destroyer *Wakaba* in Paramushiro Channel and damaged her bow. The damage was moderate, but the ship had to return to Yokosuka for repairs. This photo shows *Ikazuchi* at Yokosuka on April 12, 1943. It is estimated that the destroyer to the left is either *Michishio* or *Yamagumo*. The heavy cruiser is *Maya*, and the destroyer to the right is *Shirayuki*, *Akebono*, or *Ushio*. *Kure Maritime Museum*

On September 5, 1944, *Hibiki* departed Takao, Formosa, to escort a convoy to Manila. The next day, she was seriously damaged by a US submarine (possibly *Hake*) as she was trying to assist the sinking transport *Eiji Maru*. *Hibiki* was hit forward of the bridge, and the bow was nearly severed. The ship returned to Takao for repairs, and it was discovered that she had a 5-meter-long breach near the waterline and below the no. 1 gun mount. This photo was taken at Takao on October 6, 1944. *Hibiki* was docked at Yokosuka for repairs on November 16.

Hibiki with torpedo damage at Takao, Formosa, on October 6, 1944. In this photo, the damaged bow portion has been lifted to its original position. Note the breach near the waterline below the removed no. 1 gun mount. A twin 25 mm machine gun mount is installed forward of the bridge. *Kure Maritime Museum*

CHAPTER 5
Protection

Like other small warships, no direct protection—only indirect by (narrow) watertight compartments—could be provided. The fitting of a central longitudinal bulkhead in the engine rooms was, as will be stated in the next chapter, a failure, and contrary to the intention, it increased the danger. At that time, damage control was, if at all, in a rudimentary state, at best, and it was not much improved afterward.

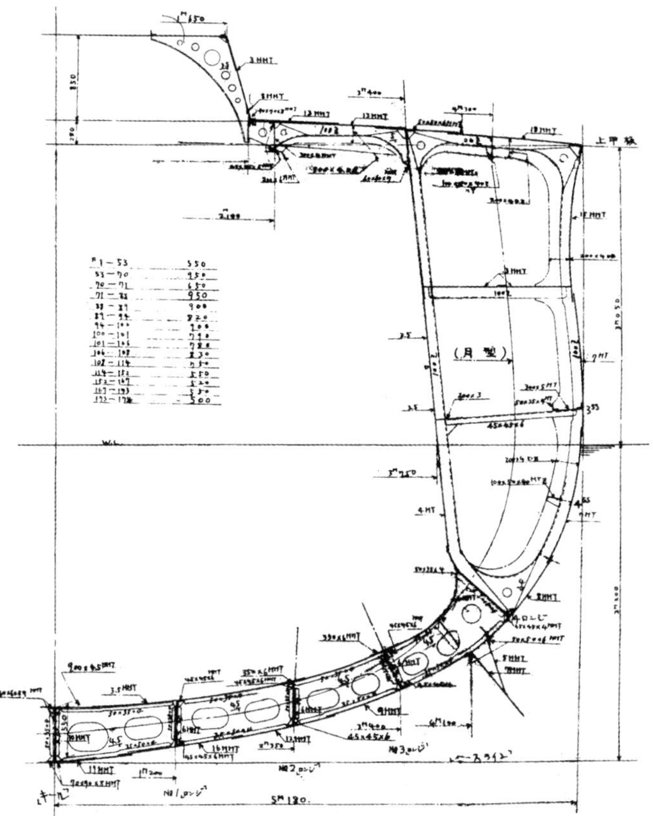

Midship section of the Fubuki-class as built.

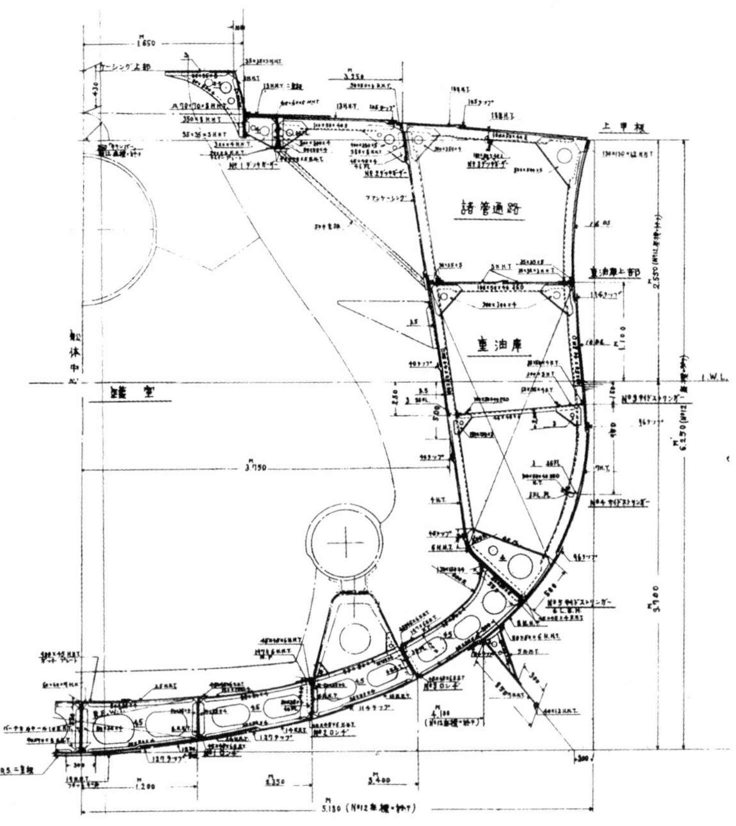

Midship section after improvement. Note the strengthening of the hull. The thickness of the outer plating was generally increased, and DS steel was used instead of HHT on some places.

CHAPTER 6

Machinery[1]

These destroyers were propelled by two sets of turbines, each consisting of one high-pressure (HPT), one low-pressure (LPT), and one simple turbine working on a two-pinion gearwheel. The designed power was 50,000 shp, with 400 rpm ahead and 10,000 shp astern. Separately, one cruising turbine (CRT) was connected to the simple turbine by a cruising reduction gear. The turbines were all of the Kampon impulse type. The number of stages and bucket rows in each stage is shown in the following table.

Stages/turbine	CRT	Simple turbine	HPT	LPT
First stage	I 2	I 1	I 1	I 1
Second stage	I 1	I 1	I 1	I 1
Third stage	I 1	I 1	I 1	I 1
Fourth stage	I 1	I 1	I 1	I 1
Fifth stage		I 1		I 1
Sixth stage		I 1		
Seventh stage		I 1		
Astern turbine		I 3		

Note:
I = impulse; 1, 2, 3 = number of bucket rows

The turbine blades were made of stainless-steel B (*otsu*), except those of the first stage, first row, for which stainless-steel A (*kō*) was used.

The angle of the nozzles was initially planned to be 12° but was actually made 14°. By this increase of the angle at the outlet, a better result was achieved. Therefore, this change was followed in *Miyuki*, *Murakumo*, and *Uranami*.

For the ships whose construction was started after 1927, the adoption of an integrated type of nozzle at the high-pressure parts was decided on. Those parts had a comparatively low nozzle height, but the speed of the steam was at the highest rate, and this type was adopted to obtain an exact nozzle area and angle. This type of nozzle was experimentally fitted to the first stages of the simple turbine and the cruising turbine.

This class, for the first time, adopted the natural flow of seawater to the condenser. The result was quite satisfactory because a sufficient amount of seawater was delivered by opening the seawater suction valve for only one-quarter of the schedule at the trials of *Uranami* and *Miyuki* and also at the high-speed-range (radius of action) trial of *Hatsuyuki*. Therefore, the designed area of the seawater suction and exhaust pipes could be reduced to about 64% after *Oboro*.

Several years earlier, Kampon had designed a propeller shaft bearing, and Hiro Naval Yard (N.Y.) tested it for a long time, with eventually favorable results. Therefore Hiro N.Y. finished the tests, and *Hatsuyuki* and *Uranami* were the first to be fitted with this Kampon type of shaft bearing.

The steam for the operation of the turbines was provided by four *Ro Gō* Kampon-type oil-burning water tube boilers without superheater. The steam pressure was 20 kg/cm^2, and it was reduced to 17 kg/cm^2 at the turbine inlet. Saturated steam was used. The boilers were fitted with six down tubes forward and six aft. The oil burners were thirteen units of 500 kg/hour and two units of 300 kg/hour capacity, making a total of 7,100 kg/hour.

In 1930, tests were performed with #2 cone at #1 burner, using *Shikinami*, and the result was "excellent." Therefore, the sister ships and the heavy cruisers *Ashigara*, *Haguro*, and *Furutaka* also changed the cones to this type.

The air for the boiler rooms was suctioned from the ventilator cowls built around the funnels (see “General Arrangement”), and this method proved effective not only for the preheating of the air but also for the prevention of spray and breaking seas, thus contributing remarkably to the increase in boiler efficiency.

As stated above, the Fubuki class was built in three groups. The types and structures of the turbines were the same in all ships, but as for the boilers, there were the following differences:

- The air preheater was test-produced in Maizuru N.Y. after 1928-equipped *Sazanami*, the last completed ship of the second group built there. The tests resulted in a reduction of fuel consumption in the range of about 15% and 10% at low and high speeds, respectively. Furthermore, the weight of the boiler could be reduced by about 10%. For the steam drums and the water drum, seamless tubes were used.

- On the basis of the result for *Sazanami*, the four ships of the third group (*Akatsuki*, *Hibiki*, *Ikazuchi*, and *Isonami*) had one boiler less (three units) by fitting an air preheater. Consequently, the weight of the boilers was reduced by 23% (58 tons) compared to the ships fitted with four boilers. The fuel consumption was reduced by 14% at full speed, and the radius of action obtained by burning 1 ton of fuel was increased by 7%.

The arrangement of the turbines and boilers and their use were as follows:

a) CRT, simple turbine	=	Up to 18 knots: combined use of CRT and simple turbine
b) Simple turbine	=	More than 18 knots, up to 24 knots
c) Simple turbine, HPT, LPT	=	More than 24 knots

What deserves attention is the attempt to reduce fuel consumption at low speed by the aforementioned connections. Also, the mounting of a cruising turbine was a “first” in a destroyer propulsion system.

The engine rooms were divided by a longitudinal bulkhead at the centerline, and the auxiliary machinery room was separated. The designers wanted to locally restrict the effect of damage and to make sure that one turbine set would remain operable if the other one failed. But this arrangement had the flaw of significantly increasing a list caused by flooding in case of damage to one side, and, since the reserve buoyancy of such small ships was correspondingly small, of increasing the danger of capsizing. Consequently, in the next class, the Hatsuharu, the central bulkhead was abolished, and the Fubuki class was the only destroyer class with this layout.

After *Shikinami*, an electrically driven hydraulic steering gear was adopted, instead of the previous steam-operated one, and telemotors were fitted.

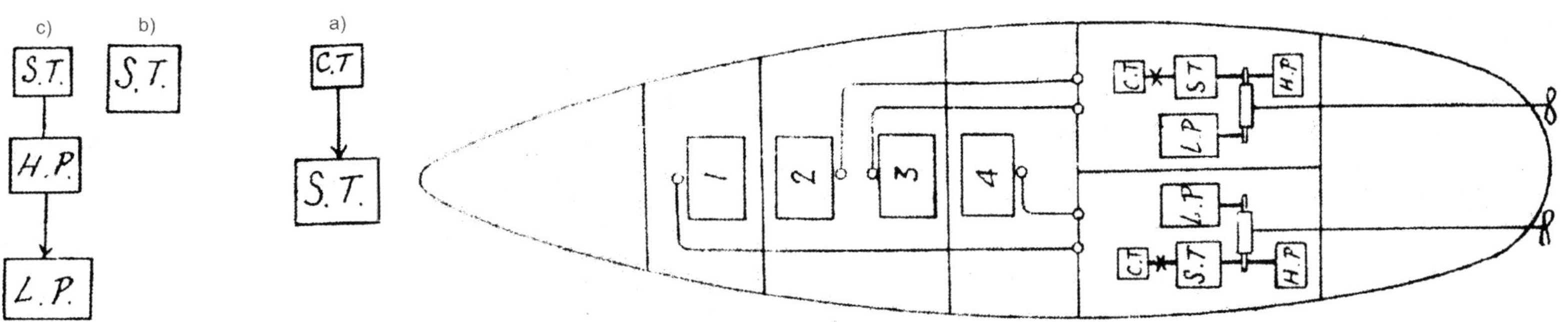

Left: *Asagiri*’s arrangement of turbines and their use. *Right*: *Asagiri*’s machinery layout: 1, 2, 3, 4 = boilers; C.T. = cruising turbine; S.T. = simple turbine; L.P. = low-pressure turbine; H.P. = high-pressure turbine; × = cruising reduction gear; ☐ = main reduction gear. *Kaigun Kikanshi*

Outline of the Trial Results of the Destroyer *Isonami*						
Condition	Speed	rpm Shaft	Shp	Steam consumption, shp/h (kg)	Fuel consumption, shp/h (kg)	Number of boilers in operation
Full power, closed	37.4	417.97	53,811		0.464	4
Full power, open	37.1	413.81	52,121		0.480	4
4/10 full power, open	28.97	287.75	21,656		0.540	3
Cruising full power, open	17.764	164.88	3,594		0.946	1
14 knots, open	14.183	128.5	1,711		0.814	1
Astern full power	?	237.5	10,533		?	4

Note:
The designed rpm of each turbine were
HPT = 3,382
LPT = 2,657
CRT = 4,704 (simple turbine + CRT combined full power)
Simple turbine = 2,657
AST = 1,562

Fubuki attained 37.98 knots with 50,691 shp and 2,028.5 tonnes of displacement. Propulsion efficiency was not good—in fact, reaching only 46% to 48%, it was poor beyond imagination! The reason was the insufficient depth of the propellers. They were fitted too shallow, and this resulted in insufficient tip clearance (i.e., the distance between the outer hull plating and the propeller tip was about 16% of the propeller diameter, and this was too small). This defect was discovered in the cavitation tunnel at the Naval Technical Research Institute during the stern knuckle experiments when designing the destroyers of the Kagerō class. By the way, the diameter of the propellers was 3.20 meters, and the pitch was 3.70 meters.

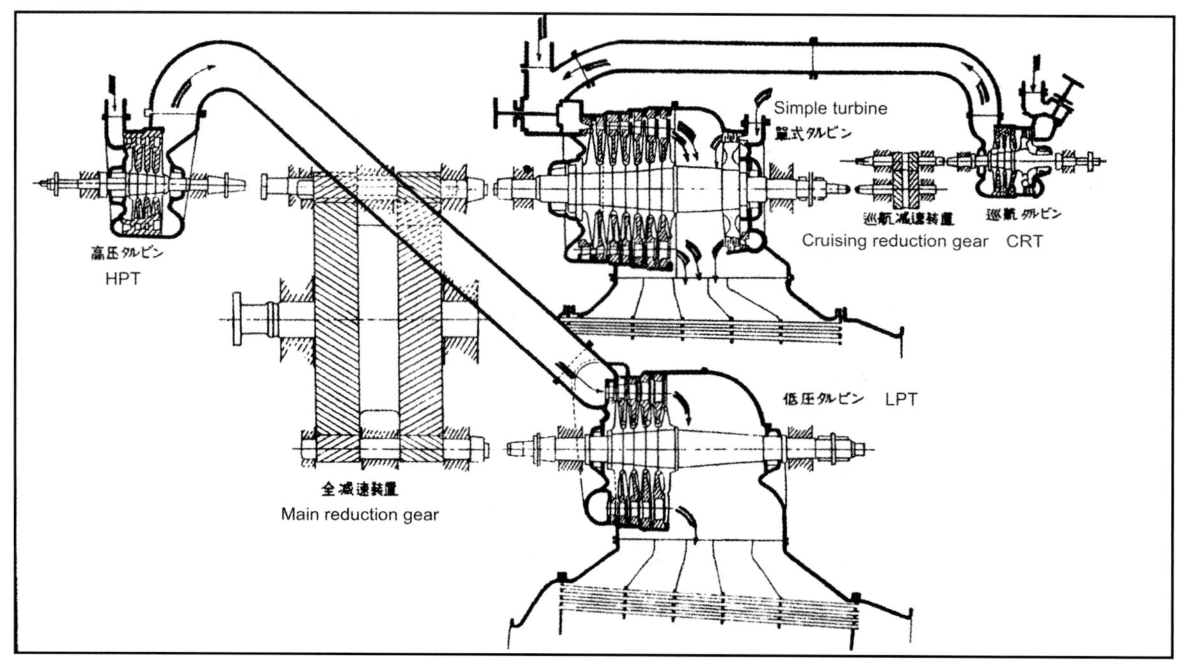

Arrangement with simple turbine (designed by Shibuya Ryūtarō) of the Fubuki class. *Kaigun Kikanshi*

Fukuda Keiji, in *Gunkan Kihon Keikaku Shiryō* ("Outline of the fundamental design of warships"), gives a figure of 47% as an average value for this class after reconstruction with 23,500 ehp and 50,000 shp (p. 116). The trial result for *Shirakumo* at 2,473.8 tonnes was the following: a speed of 34.91 knots, 50,257 shp at 394 rpm (stated as 24,830 ehp), and 49.4% propulsion efficiency. For *Shirayuki*, the following values are noted: a speed of 18 knots, 4,500 shp, 2,260 tank ehp, and 50.2% propulsion efficiency.

Makino Shigeru, in his *Makino Shigeru Kansen Nōto* ("Makino Shigeru's notes about warships"), states that "the dissatisfaction after entering service was the small range," but if the values provided by Fukuda are correct, his critique is hard to understand, because the Naval General Staff required 4,000 nm, and this range was attained. But Makino may have referred to the "expectations" of the Naval General Staff (5,000 nm).[2]

Range (Radius of Action) of *Hatsuyuki*

Item/condition	As completed	As refitted (1)	As refitted (2)
Displacement (tonnes)	1,989	2,509	2,440
Speed (knots)	13,456	14,404	14
Range (nm)	4,875	4,095	5,100
Shp	1,658	1,908	1,900
Propulsion coefficient (PC)	?	0.498	?
Fuel consumption. shp/hr.	0.79	?	0.766
Fuel (tons)	449.1	538.8	552.81

Source:
Fukuda, *Gunkan Kihon Keikaku Shiryō*, 121.

The following tables provide some more data in reference to machinery:

Turning Circle of *Uranami*

Displacement	Speed	Am/Ar	DT/L	Heel angle
1,943	34.58	49.66	8.03	8
2,472	32.50	61.6	7.67	11

Notes:
Am = lateral middle line area; Ar = rudder area; DT = transfer; L = length

Source:
Fukuda, *Gunkan Kihon Keikaku Shiryō*, 124.

Electric Generators

Name/item	Displacement	Diesel	Turbine	Total
Fubuki (after refitting)	2,466 tonnes	1 × 40 kW	2 × 33 kW	106 kW
Akatsuki	2,430 tonnes	1 × 25 kW	2 × 55 kW	135 kW

Fubuki during trials off Miyazu Bay in the summer of 1928. This is an official photo taken by the Maizuru Construction Department (*kōsakubu*), a yard specialized in destroyer construction.

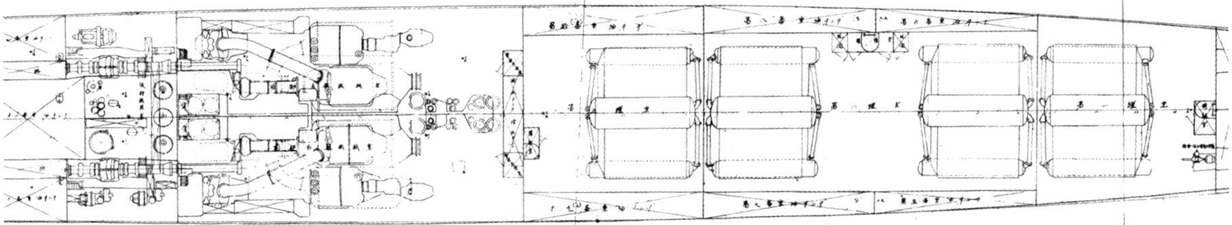

Machinery spaces of the *Uranami* after improvement

Shirakumo at speed, with sister *Shinonome* beyond, on August 31, 1931. The special-type destroyers had two sets of turbines with a designed output of 50,000 shp. During trials, *Shirakumo* attained a speed of 34.91 knots with an output of 50,257 shp.

Shikinami during trials off Miyazu on November 13, 1929. This is a builder's photo by Maizuru Naval Station, Construction Department (Yōkōbu Kōsakubu). The sea is quite high and the smoke emission is quite dense, indicating that boiler operation has not yet reached perfection. *Shikinami* had a displacement of 2,013 tons, and with 51,100 shp she attained 37.93 knots. Note that she had shielded torpedo mounts from completion.

Yūgiri pictured during trials on November 29, 1930, off Miyazu. It is a builder's photo taken only four days before delivery. In this trial, not only the performance of the machinery but also the capability to produce black smoke was tested, by incompletely burning heavy oil and making a smoke screen.

Sagiri was the last destroyer of the "fog group" and was completed at Uraga Dock on January 31, 1931. This picture shows her during trials off Tateyama in late 1930. The ship is moving fast and is turning slightly to port, so the hull is leaning to starboard. Note the "mushroom type" ventilators beside the funnels. This was a distinction of the second and third groups of the special type—and *Uranami. The Maru Special*

CHAPTER 7

Armament

The predecessor of the Fubuki class, the Mutsuki class, included the first destroyers mounting 61 cm torpedoes ("eight-year-type no. 2") and "twelve-year-type triple" above water torpedo tubes. These torpedo tubes were designed and produced by Aichi Dokei (Clock) Company and the Watanabe Ironworks (Tekkōsho), which also manufactured the successor, modification 1. In response to the requirement of the Naval General Staff, three triple torpedo tubes of this type were mounted on the centerline. This enabled the simultaneous launching of nine torpedo "lines" (the Mutsuki class had six lines). It was the most powerful torpedo armament mounted on any destroyer at that time. The main differences between the basic torpedo tube and the modified version were the revision of one part of the storage system of the high-pressure air system for launching the torpedoes, dispensing with the spare gear, and a few changes to the dimensions. This is shown in the next table.

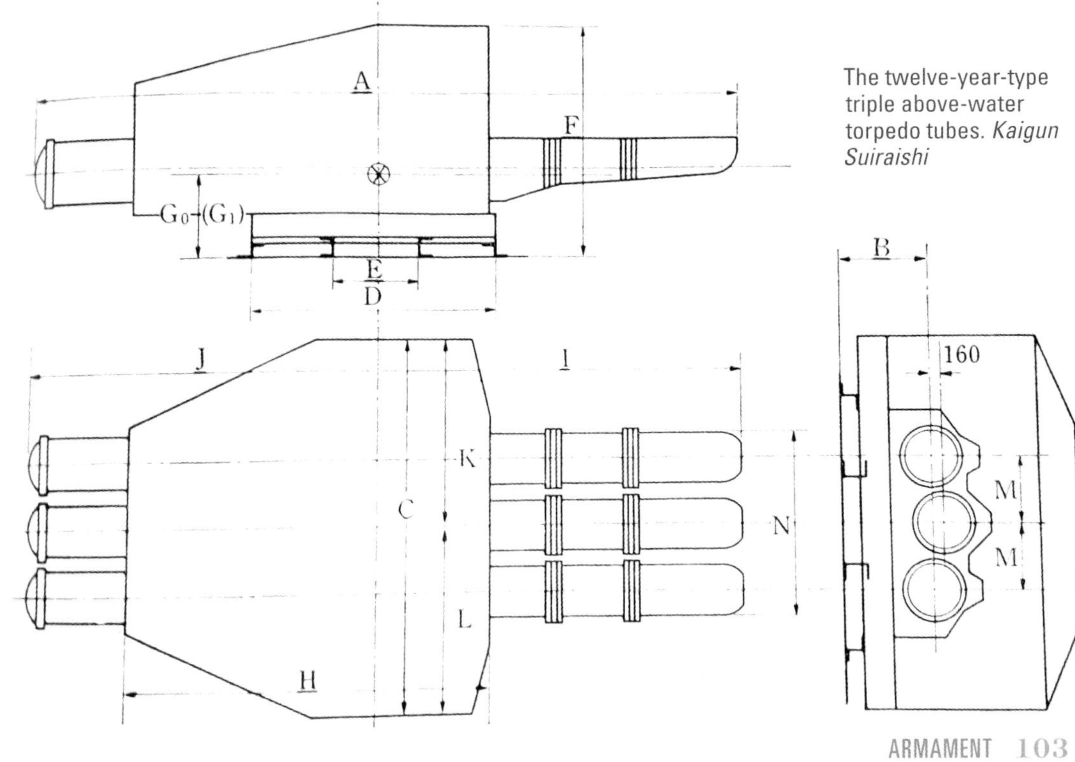

The twelve-year-type triple above-water torpedo tubes. *Kaigun Suiraishi*

Item/type	Twelve-year-type triple TTs	Twelve-year-type triple TTs, mod. 1
Length (mm)	8,803	8,503
Height of center of the TT (mm)	908	908
Maximum width of shield (mm)	4,239	4,239
Diameter of training platform (mm)	2,975	2,975
Diameter of the (training) axis (mm)	1,055	1,005
Height of shield (mm)	2,708	2,708
Position of CG (unloaded) (mm)	825	approx. 825
Position of CG (loaded) (mm)	863	approx. 863
Length of shield (mm)	4,225	4,225
Distance from the center of axis to the fore end of spoon (mm)	4,545	4,545
Distance from the center of axis to the rear end of tube (mm)	3,958	3,958
Distance from the center of axis to the left side (mm)	2,164	2,164
Distance from the center of axis to the right side (mm)	2,075	2,075
Distance between the centerlines of neighboring tubes (mm)	780	780
Width of the tubes (mm)	2,353	2,353
Training gear	Manual and mechanical (spare gear)	Manual and mechanical
Performance of the Janney-type electrohydraulic training motor (hp)	5	5
Rpm of the training motor	500	500
Voltage	100	100
Time for training 360°, manual and mechanical (s)	35 and 23	35 and 23
Time for launching the torpedoes (s)	18	18
Minimum distance between running torpedoes (mm)	4.5	4.5
Weight of the TT (tons)	13,500	13,850
Weight of the shield (tons)	1,900	1,900
Weight of related parts (tons)	0.150	0.150
Total weight (tons)	15,550	15,900
Fitted on	Mutsuki class	Fubuki class

Source:
Kaigun Suiraishi Kankōkai, *Kaigun Suiraishi* ("History of the naval underwater weapons") (Tokyo: Shinkōsha, 1979), 206.

Note:
CG = center of gravity

The shield was mounted to protect the crew from weather influences and to ascertain communication. At the same time, it provided some splinter protection. The fitting of the shield was comparable to the use of closed gunhouses and was very effective, and it was used not only in succeeding torpedo tube types but also on those already mounted aboard the Mutsuki class. While the third group was completed with shields already in place, the first twenty ships were completed without them, and shields were fitted afterward.

A skid beam reloading system was fitted to increase the torpedo power and fulfill the purpose despite its incompleteness when compared with the later-introduced quick-reloading system. When compared to the former system (transportation by carriage), it was a big improvement and provided much more safety to the handlers.

The torpedoes were always of the 61 cm type, at first consisting of eighteen of the eight-year type and then, after refitting, eighteen of the type 90 and, after 1939, eighteen[1] of the oxygen-propelled type 93.[2] Nine torpedoes were in the torpedo tubes, and the spare torpedoes were placed on either side of the second funnel to port of the no. 2 main gun.

The following table provides some principal data of the main armament.

compressors. In 1914, the *Bu*- and *U*-type compressors were test-produced by that company and Ishikawajima Shipyard. In the following year, Kōbe Seikō concluded a contract with the British Peter Brotherhood Company and received the license of the high-pressure air compressor of that company. In 1916–17, Kōbe Seikō began production of the Y 6 type, which was based on this. This type was mounted not only on the Fubuki class but also on several other destroyers.[3] Y 6 was of the vertical, steam-engine-driven, four-stage-compression, direct-connecting type (i.e., above the vertical engine, each stage of air cylinder was directly connected). This type could produce 720 liters of compressed air at 250 kg/cm^2 pressure in one hour. The engine operated with 11 kg/cm^2 steam pressure at 350 rpm, and the weight was 1.98 tons. A slightly modified type (Kai 1) was mounted on *Oboro* and *Akebono*. It differed from the original type in its higher pressure (300 kg/cm^2), increased rpm (500), and lesser weight (1.60 tons). After *Sazanami*, the W 8–type modification 1 was mounted. It had the same pressure as the Y 6–type modification 1 but produced 900 liters per hour of compressed air in five compression stages; consequently it weighted more (2 tonnes).

Principal Data of Main Armament

Item/type	Eight-year type	Type 90	Type 93, model 1
Length (m)	8.415	8.550	9.000
Weight (kg)	2,400	2,540	2.765
Main engine	Four cylinder, radial (German Schwartzkopff type)	Two cylinder, reciprocating (British Whitehead type)	Two cylinder, double acting, wet heater, 100% oxygen, seawater diluent (improved Whitehead design)
Air pressure (kg/cm^2)	195	225	225
Explosive weight (kg)	345	400	492
Tail structure	Woolwich	?	Woolwich-type fins and rudders
Speed and range (knots/m)	38/10,000	46/7,000	48/22,000
	32/15,000	42/10,000	40/32,000
	27/20,000	35/15,000	36/40,000

The volume of the air chamber of the eight-year-type torpedo was 1,081 liters, and the pressure was 195 kg/cm^2; for filling the air chamber, an air compressor was necessary. The IJN imported the air compressor together with the torpedo: first from Germany, then from France, and thereafter from Britain. After the Russo-Japanese War (1904–05), a need for domestic manufacture was urgently felt, and Kōbe Seikō was ordered to produce the air

In concert with the change to the oxygen-driven torpedo, it became necessary to fill the chamber with pure oxygen. The chamber of the type 93 torpedo had a volume of 980 liters of oxygen at 225 kg/cm^2. The first trials with the type 93 generator were not satisfactory, so the IJN switched to the secondary air compressor type 5.[4] This type, known as the type 95 generator within the IJN, had a capacity of 15 m^3/h[5] and was designed and produced by the former Japan Oxygen Company, founded in 1910 as Japan's first industrial plant in this field. This compressor was mounted on the Fubuki class in 1941–42 and on the destroyers completed afterward.

The Navy Technical Department had ordered the company to produce the oxygen compressor in 1932 in conjunction with the development of the oxygen torpedo. Then Japan Oxygen Company planned domestic production of the distillation-type oxygen separator and referred to authorities of Tōhoku University, but it was only after the involvement of Mr. Moma Gohei in April 1934 that the design progressed and the following characteristics were fulfilled: (1) lightweight and small volume, (2) low height, and (3) maintaining more than 98% purity, irrespective of the rolling and pitching of the ship.[6] The functioning principle was the separation of air into oxygen and nitrogen. The compressor air (therefore, the ship still needed an air compressor) was jetted out from the nozzle, and the gas liquefied. In the generator (column), the temperature difference was used for the separation of the oxygen and the nitrogen by evaporation. The oxygen plant was composed of several parts, and the fission of the air occurred in the heat exchanger and rectification (or distillation) column, which were combined into one outer casing. The column was divided into three main parts: lower column, condenser, and upper column. New ideas referring to the shape and arrangement of the distillation plates, an increase in the diameter of the distillation pipes, a reduction in the distillation power to a minimum if necessary, etc. were introduced and registered as secret patents by the IJN. As an example, there were nine plates in the lower, copper column, and twenty-five in the upper one, made of the same material, while for the condenser in between, brass was used. The plates consisted of flat brass discs perforated with a large number of 0.9 mm holes. The surface of each was divided into sections by copper partitions 9 mm high. In the lower column, these partitions ran at right angles to each other and divided the surface of a plate into about 40 sections, as seen in the image at right.

In the upper column the partitions had a wavy form, and they divided the surface into about 400 sections, as shown in the image at right.

By this design, the plate surfaces remained covered with refluxing liquid even when the column was not exactly vertical, and this was the reason why sufficient pure oxygen was obtained up to 5° inclination.[7] Also, each plate was covered with a corrugated brass plate that had been stamped with a large number of slotted holes to increase contact between the ascending gas and the reflux, as shown in the figures. The reflux could flow from one plate to the next by means of four connecting copper pipes, which ran from each plate to the one below. At the top of the column, above the liquid nitrogen reflux inlet, about 6,000 brass Raschig rings were packed.

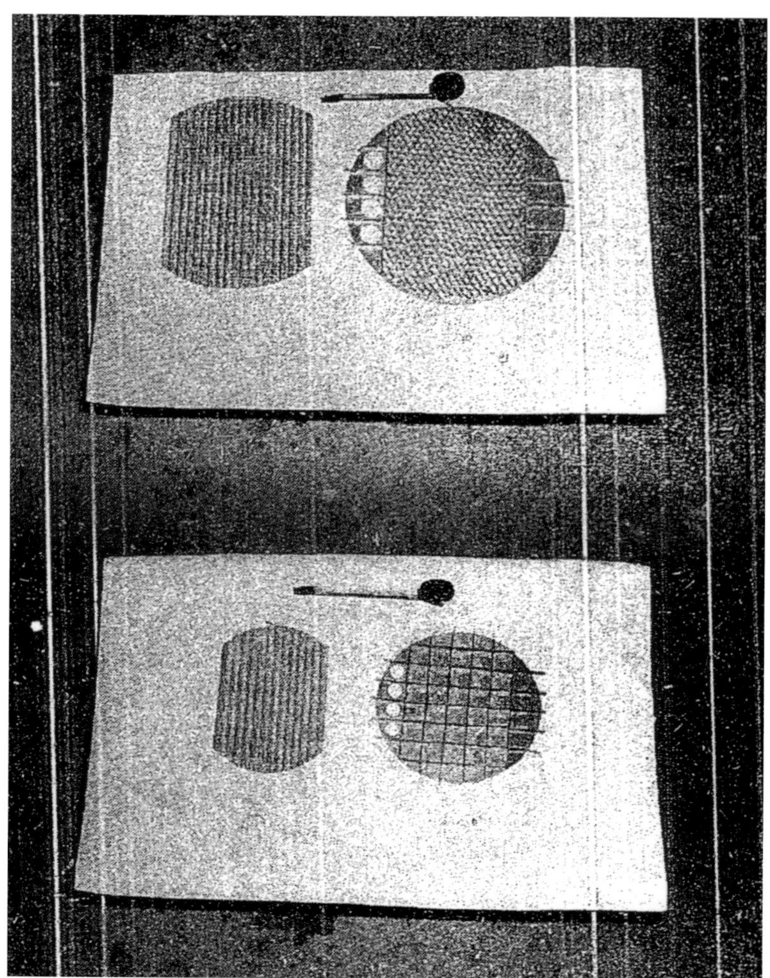

TOP: Plate of upper column.
BOTTOM: Plate of lower column. *US Naval Technical Mission to Japan*

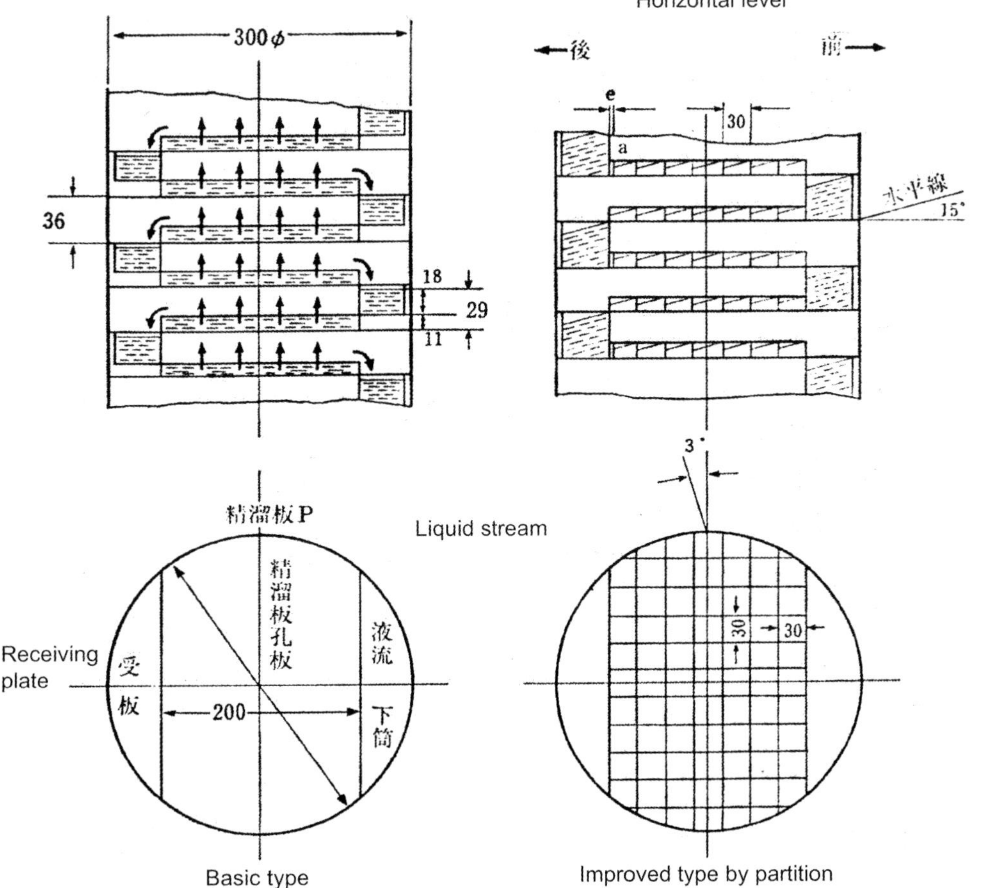

In the case of the separation being vertical, rectification plate with holes. The ideas represented by the two types were registered as secret patents for the IJN. *Kaigun Suiraishi*

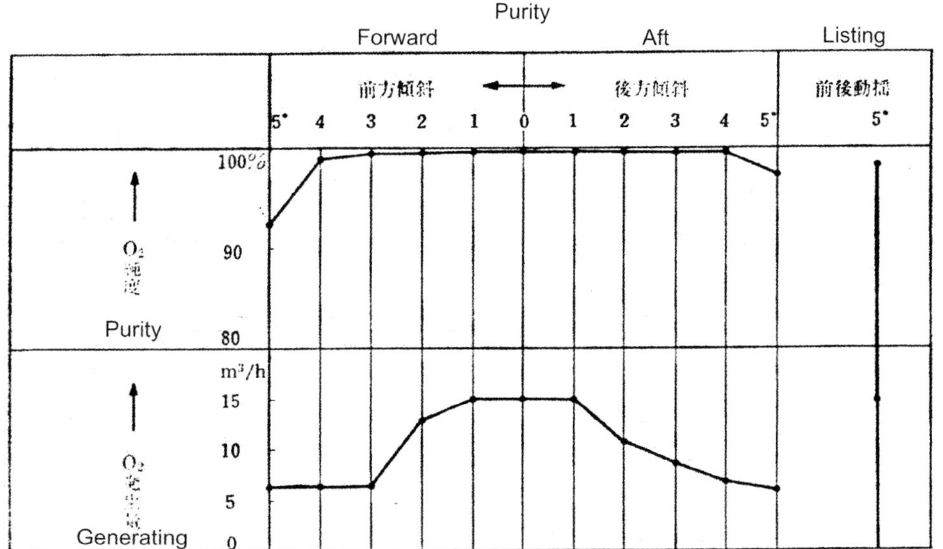

Secondary air compressor type 5 (15 m^3) (special-use separator). Test for listing and plane. *Kaigun Suiraishi*

Plan view of the evaporator located in the bottom of the lower column. *US Naval Technical Mission to Japan*

Shown above is a plan view of the generator located in the bottom of the lower column, and at right is a general view of the column, generating the free oxygen.

In order to fill it into the chamber of the torpedo, an oxygen compressor pump, called the second air pressure pump, was necessary. Mitsui Seiki Kōgyō KK began the design and production in 1936 by order of the IJN. But the compression of the high-purity oxygen, 250 kg/cm^2, involved a substantial danger of explosion. Extreme care was necessary to select the materials, and the company used copper alloy and high-nickel stainless steel for the cylinders and piston valves to avoid corrosion. Also, the cooling and lubricating systems had to be adapted for the use of oxygen. After some tests, a compression of up to 250 kg/cm^2 could be attained during trials, and then "mass production" for destroyers and other warship types equipped with the "oxygen separator" (as the column was commonly known) was decided on. For destroyers, the type 2 pump was used (other ship types used the type 4 with 30 m^3/h capacity of free oxygen). The highest working pressure was 300 kg/cm^2, with a capacity of free oxygen at 15 m^3/hour, and the electric motor delivered 20 hp at 600 rpm.

Finally, the image opposite shows the oxygen flow diagrammatically, and it gives a good overview of this rather dangerous process. By the way, the weight of smaller marine-type oxygen plants for destroyers was approximately 8 tons.

The fire control system (*hasshashikisōchi*) at first consisted of two fire directors of type 14, but this was later modified to two type 91, model 2 fire directors (*hōiban*) and two type 91 fire command panels (*hasshashikiban*).

General view of the rectifying column. *US Naval Technical Mission to Japan*

To obtain the firing angle of the torpedo during the Taishō period (1912–1926), the IJN used very simple fire directors such as the four-year, eight-year, and 14-year types. Fitted with 5 cm binoculars, these directors were designed by the Second Division of the Navy Technical Department and were manufactured in navy yards. They were fitted on heavy and light cruisers and on destroyers.

Early in the Shōwa era, Japan Optical Company (Nihon Kōgaku—nowadays Nikon) was charged with the development of torpedo fire control systems. The first product of the cooperation between the Navy Technical Department and this company was the type 90 fire director, fitted with 6 cm binoculars and capable of calculating the target-bearing angle. In the following year, 1931, they started production of the type 91 fire director. Once more, it was a joint venture together with the Navy Technical Department (fundamental design). The Navy Technical Department was

Oxygen flow diagram. *US Naval Technical Mission to Japan*

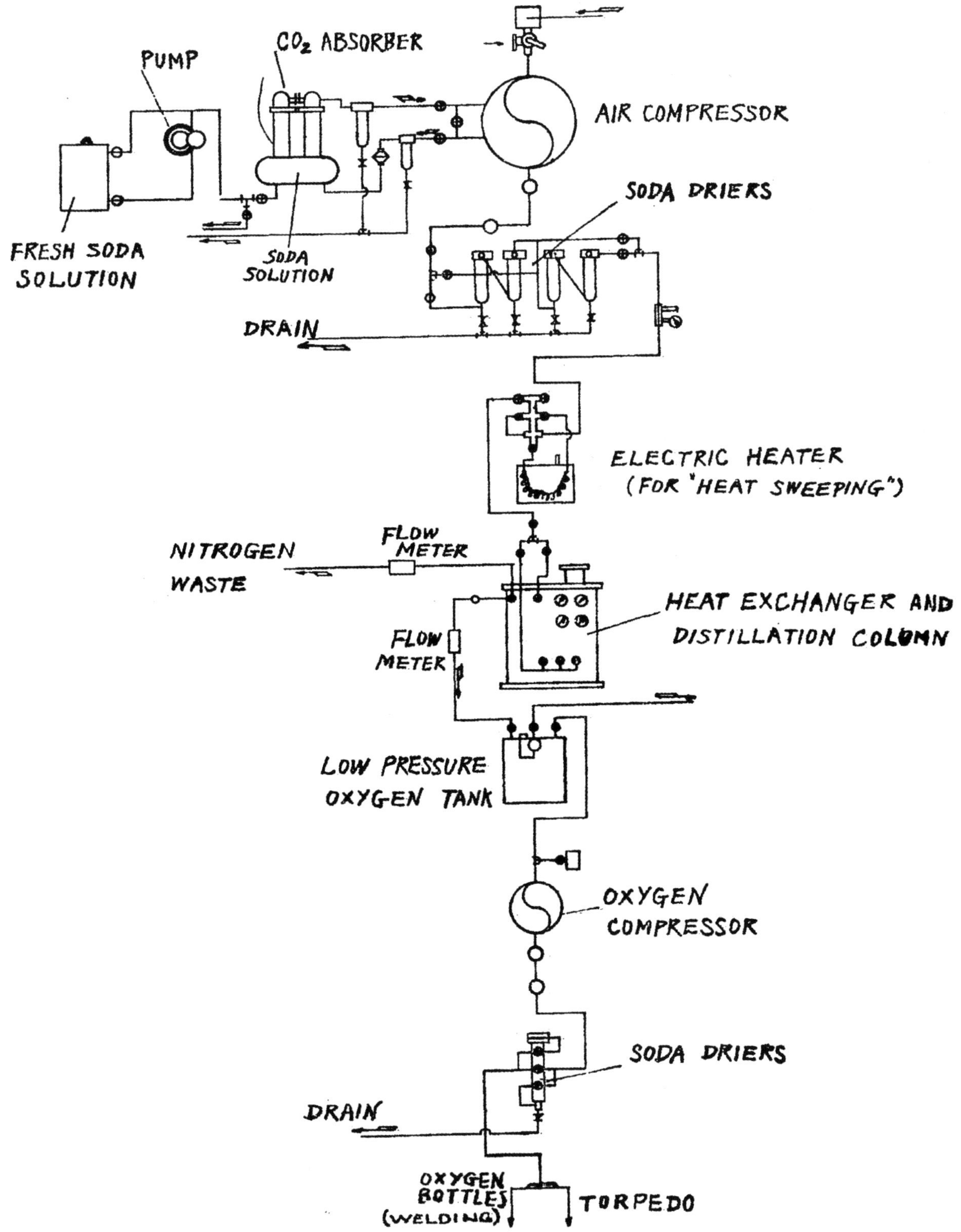

represented by Lt. Cmdr. (later captain) Norita Kiyoshi and engineer Kazunori Sunosuke, and the Japan Optical Company by engineers Murata and Yanagishira as the main responsible designers (detailed design). Three models were produced, fitted with either 8 cm or 12 cm binoculars and capable of transmitting the oblique angle (gyro angle) continuously to the torpedo tubes. About 120 units were produced and fitted on surface vessels fitted with torpedo tubes, such as destroyers, light cruisers, and heavy cruisers.

A Vickers Company torpedo fire director was bought by the IJN in 1931, and it promoted the progress of the torpedo fire control systems. Together with the improvement of the fire director, the fire command panel and the communication system were added, while in response to increased battle ranges, the binoculars were further enlarged. The first fire command panel was the type 92 *hasshashikiban*, whose production was planned for 1932. In the Navy Technical Department, the same persons were in charge of the fundamental design, but the Japan Optical Company was represented by engineers Ninomiya, Ishiwara, and Nakayama. The panel was fitted with either 12 cm or 15 cm binoculars, and atop the column, placed on an antivibration platform, was mounted a subcompass. Various inputs could be made to the different rings, and this instrument delivered gyro-correction angles and launching-angle corrections. As stated above, the 12 cm binoculars were changed to the 15 cm type, but aside from this, about 215 identical units were produced over a period of about ten years, with "mass production" starting in 1935.

In the same year, the production of the type 93 computer model 2 (*93 Shiki shahōban ni gata*) was decided on, but for reasons unknown to the authors, production stopped after about six units. It was a calculation instrument for destroyers, and it was used in combination with the type 91 fire director. By plotting the target and one's own ship's positions continuously, the torpedo-tube-training angle was transmitted and indirect torpedo launching was permitted. This computer was replaced by the type 97, model 2, of which fifty-six units for destroyers were completed, but according to sources available to the authors, it was never fitted on the Fubuki class—only on the most-modern fleet-type destroyers.

Therefore, in the end the Fubuki class fought with an already outdated torpedo fire control system in the Pacific war, despite the mounting of type 93 oxygen torpedoes and despite the fact that they had the most powerful torpedo armament among the Japanese destroyers, with the exception of the experimental *Shimakaze* (II).

The heavy-artillery armament was comparable to the powerful torpedo armament and consisted of six 50 cal., three-year-type, 12.7 cm low-angle guns in three twin mounts. The adoption of twin turret-like gun mounts was big progress compared to the previous single 12 cm deck gun on a pedestal mount; in particular the employment of gunhouses was a new approach. The increased caliber had been required by the Navy General Staff because they feared that foreign navies would adopt it for their new destroyers,[8] and the gunhouses permitted their use independently of weather conditions. One mount was placed on the long forecastle forward of the bridge, and two were arranged aft. The second gun was located on the aft deckhouse and was superimposed to the third one, placed farther aft on the upper deck. This was a novel arrangement, and it was first adopted for the Fubuki class. This arrangement was continued for successive destroyer classes, after a short intermezzo of a vice versa arrangement in the Hatsuharu and Shiratsuyu classes, which required reconstruction after the "*Tomozuru* accident."[9]

The first group was equipped with gun mounts of model A, with 40° elevation and both guns fixed in a common cradle. The mount was trained on a comparatively simple turntable, using an electrohydraulic transmission gear. The gunhouse was made of only 3.2 mm thick steel plates and protected the crew only against wind and waves. The ammunition supply was manual from below.[10] Because of this rather simple design, weight, volume, and also the diameter of the turntable were comparatively small.

When *Ayanami* was being "designed," the adoption of the 40 cal., type 89, 12.7 cm, twin high-angle gun was considered, but this was given up in favor of the model B gun mount, characterized by the independent movement of the guns and the change of the elevation angle to 75°, to enable its use as a dual-purpose weapon. The dimensions of the carriages and the gunhouse were increased considerably, and the diameter of the turntable also became bigger. The ammunition handling was also improved, and hoists were fitted. The weight increased by about 30% and became about 32 tons. However, irrespective of these improvements, the gun was practically useless as a high-angle gun because no high-angle fire control system was fitted, and the rate of fire was too low.

The principal technical data are shown in the following table.

Principal Technical Data	
Bore, nominal/actual	12.7 cm (5")/same
Barrel length	50 cal. (6.35 m)
Breech, type and mechanism	Welin screw, normal swinging
Construction	Built-up, radially expanded (autofrettage)
Rifling	Uniform (one turn in 28 calibers)
Maximum bore pressure	28.4 kg/cm²
Weight including breech	4.205 tons
Life of the gun barrel	approx. 550 rounds
Maximum elevation and depression angles	+40° to –7° (model A); +75° to –7° (model B)
Training and elevation speeds	4°–6°/s and 6°12'/s, respectively, by cylindrical worm and worm wheel gear
Training and elevating method	Follow the pointer (using electrohydraulic drives)
Turntable	Fabricated; training on equidistantly spaced rollers in roller path
Projectile hoists	Pusher type from magazine to gunhouse
Supply rate	10 projectiles and 10 powder bags
Weight of projectiles	23.5 kg (common, incendiary shrapnel [antiaircraft use], illumination); 21 kg for antisubmarine
Weight of charge	7.25–7.67 kg
Muzzle velocity	910 m/s (often stated as 915 m/s)
Fuse setting and ramming	Manual on loading tray before ramming by hand
Rate of fire	5 rounds/min. (also stated as 4.4 rounds/min.)
Gun crew	13 men (model A); 16 men (model B)
Ranges	5° = 7,235 m; 10° = 10,190 m; 20° = 14,068 m; 30° = 16,672 m;
	40° = 18,269 m; maximum vertical, 11,382 / 12,550 m
Weight of the turret	25.4 tons (model A); 32 tons (model B)
Performance	Good; less dispersion of salvo was requested
Problems	As a whole, the strength of the turret structure was considered to be inadequate

Sources:
Umi to Sora ("Sea and sky") (Kōbe, Japan: Jishūkai, Jun. 1958), 49; Yamamoto Yoshihide et al., *Nihon Kaigun Kansai Heiki Daizukan* ("All about Japanese naval shipboard weapons") (Tokyo: KK Bestsellers, 2002), 86–89; *Kaigun Hōjutsushi* ("History of naval gunnery") (Tokyo: Kaigun Hōjutsushi Kankōkai, 1975), 28 (states firing rate as "about 20 rounds/min."); and US Naval Technical Mission t5o Japan, Report 0-47(N)-1, pp. 11–23.

Together with the change of turret to model B in *Ayanami*, the fire command station and the fire director were separated and the latter was fitted in an independent tower, located above and aft of the command station. In the third (*Akatsuki*) group, the fire command station was placed in the upper aft part of the compass bridge, as part of the so-called fire control system tower, with the torpedo fire control system station above, followed by the gun fire control system station and finally the 3-meter rangefinder atop.

The first group was to be armed with two 40 mm Vickers (*Bu*-type) water-cooled, slow-firing, and ineffective machine guns (2,000 rounds per gun), but it was changed to two 7.7 mm Vickers machine guns placed on the gun platform forward of the second funnel (aft of that funnel, the 90 cm searchlight was fitted).[11] From *Ayanami*, the smaller-caliber machine gun was replaced by the larger 12.7 mm machine gun (8,000 rounds per gun), and after the outbreak of the war, the ships were equipped with more 13 mm and also 25 mm machine guns. The longer the war lasted, the more the number of close-range antiaircraft weapons increased, particularly after the gradual removal of the aft no. 2 main gun from 1943 onward. *Ushio*, for instance, mounted four 25 mm triple, one 25 mm twin, and eight 25 mm single machine guns. This made a total of twenty-two 25 mm machine guns and six 13 mm single machine guns at the end of the war.

At first the depth-charge throwers were two type 81, but this was changed to one type 91, and in concert with this, the depth charge loading racks were replaced by one type 3. In peacetime, eighteen depth charges were to be loaded, and in wartime this number increased to thirty-six. While this number was not changed, the type was altered to type 95 when it became operable.

The hydrophone was one type 93, model 1.

Two large minesweeping gears, model 2 (*taikan shiki 2 Gata*), could be mounted on the stern, and these were also maintained after refitting, when one small minesweeping gear (model 1) was added.

At first, the rangefinders were two units of 2 meters, but this was changed to one type 90, with a 3-meter base length, and one type 14, with a 2-meter base length. The destroyers of the *Akatsuki* group mounted two units with 3-meter base length from the beginning.

The binoculars on the bridge were at first of the 8 cm type but were improved to two 12 cm ones when refitted, while the *Akatsuki* group had four 12 cm from the start.

On the upper bridge were two 30 cm Sperry-type signal searchlights, and for lighting at night, one 90 cm searchlight of the same type. When the ships were refitted, one remote-control director, model 2, for the 90 cm searchlight was mounted on a platform.

At the outset of the war, the usual degaussing coil was fitted as protection against magnetic mines.

Fubuki photographed in 1932. She belonged to the 20th Destroyer Division. The special-type destroyers were armed with twelve-year-type triple, modification 1, 61 cm torpedo tubes mounted between the funnels (one mount) and between the after funnel and the afterdeck house (two mounts). As can be seen, the mounts have no shields.

Fubuki during torpedo exercises as seen from an altitude of 200 meters. The torpedo mounts (shielded) are trained to port, and torpedo tracks can be observed. This photo was probably taken on January 17, 1940, in Bungo Channel. At this time, *Fubuki* was fitted with type 90 torpedoes, and it is highly probable that she never carried type 93 oxygen torpedoes. *Sekai no Kansen*

Shinonome about 1932. The special type had nine 61 cm torpedo tubes in three triple mounts. They also had nine spare torpedoes, and these were housed in torpedo boxes on both sides of the after funnel and to port of gun mount no. 2.

Oboro and *Akebono* (*left*) refueling from *Ondo* in Sukumo Bay on April 29, 1939. The torpedo mounts are the twelve-year-type triple, with the central tube placed 160 mm higher than the left and right ones. This can be seen on *Oboro*'s mount to the right and on *Akebono*'s to the left. Toward the stern of *Oboro*, torpedo mount no. 3 can be seen with its convex-style shield. Note the 2-meter rangefinder on top of *Oboro*'s rear rudder room (emergency rudder room). *Gakken*

Shirayuki at Kure on November 5, 1929. She was equipped with 50 cal., three-year-type, 12.7 cm twin mounts, model A. The barrels could be elevated to 40º, and the maximum range was 18,269 meters. The gunhouse weighed 24.5 tons and had a thin shield made of 3.2 mm thick steel plates for protection against the elements.

Murakumo prepared for gunnery exercises in the Inland Sea in 1930. Note that the forward 12.7 cm gun barrels are elevated to approximately 40° (i.e., their maximum elevation). *Kure Maritime Museum*

Shinonome in early 1930. The no. 3 main gunhouse (model A) is trained to starboard. Note the shield on the second torpedo mount, and the pipe-type air supply vent beside the forward funnel. This is a very good view of a first-group (*Fubuki* to *Isonami*) special-type destroyer.

The forecastle deck of *Isonami* while participating in a fleet maneuver in May 1936. The deck is rather cramped, and the model A 12.7 cm gun, with its closely spaced gun barrels, is clearly seen. The left and right barrels of this mount were mounted in the same cradle and could not be elevated individually, and this is why they were fitted so close together. The B and C models had more space between the barrels. *The Maru Special*

Ayanami at anchor around 1932. She was the first ship of the second group (*II gata*) and was equipped with model B gunhouses. The shape of the gun shield is different from that of the model A, and at 32 tons the model B weighed 8 tons more than model A. However, the maximum elevation was 75°, which enabled it to be used as a dual-purpose gun, and the gun barrels could be elevated independently. The ammunition remained unchanged.

Shikinami photographed at anchor by Hatakeyama Satarō in late 1930. Although the location is not known, it is probably Ise Bay or Tateyama. Because of the shape of the 12.7 cm model B gunhouse, the forecastle looks bigger than on the first group (*I gata*). The shell supply was 150 in peacetime and 180 in wartime. Note the 2-meter rangefinder on the top of the bridge structure.

During a transport mission between Kavieng and Rekata, *Yūgiri* was torpedoed by US submarine *Grayback* on May 16, 1943. The torpedo hit *Yūgiri*'s port bow, and it was cut and bent. However, the ship could be towed by *Amagiri* to Rabaul, where she was repaired by *Yamabiko Maru* before sailing to Japan. The photo was taken at Rabaul and shows *Yūgiri* with mantlets around her forward 12.7 cm mount, a twin 25 mm machine gun mount forward of the bridge, and a bulletproof plate around the bridge. *Gakken*

Sagiri shown between August 1940 and January 1941, when she belonged to the 20th Destroyer Division. Unfortunately, the location is unknown, but some specific repair works are being carried out. A twin 13 mm machine gun mount is fitted forward of the second funnel. Note the flat aiming room on the model B 12.7 cm gunhouse.

Close-up of *Sagiri* during an exercise in October 1941. A twin 13 mm machine gun mount can be seen forward of the second funnel; behind it, a 90 cm searchlight; and at the base, a box for spare torpedoes. On top of the bridge structure is a 2-meter rangefinder, and degaussing coils are fitted around the hull sides. The two white bands on the funnel tell us that *Sagiri* is the 2nd unit of the 20th Destroyer Division of the 3rd Destroyer Squadron. This is because just prior to the Pacific war, the rules of identification bands changed when each fleet had two destroyer squadrons instead of one.

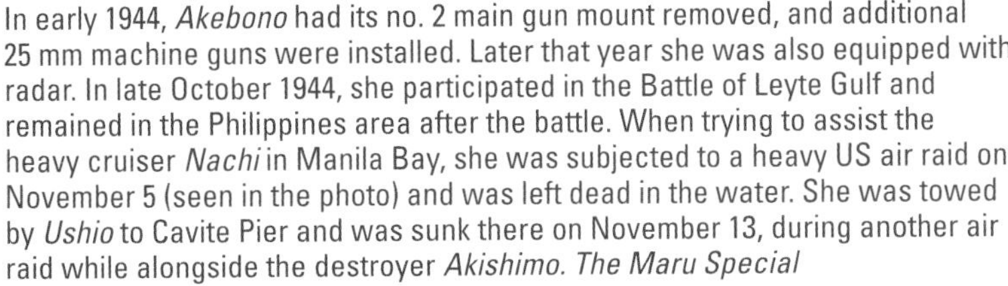

In early 1944, *Akebono* had its no. 2 main gun mount removed, and additional 25 mm machine guns were installed. Later that year she was also equipped with radar. In late October 1944, she participated in the Battle of Leyte Gulf and remained in the Philippines area after the battle. When trying to assist the heavy cruiser *Nachi* in Manila Bay, she was subjected to a heavy US air raid on November 5 (seen in the photo) and was left dead in the water. She was towed by *Ushio* to Cavite Pier and was sunk there on November 13, during another air raid while alongside the destroyer *Akishimo. The Maru Special*

Sazanami participated in the southern advance, and this is a photo taken from the heavy cruiser *Haguro* in February 1942, when *Sazanami* departed from Kendari, Celebes. Note the two parallel rows of depth charges arranged on the stern. The depth charges were placed on guide rails or on dropping stands. The stands were dropped into the sea with the depth charges. *Gakken*

Sazanami pictured from the heavy cruiser *Haguro* on February 2, 1942. In front of the second funnel, *Sazanami* has two twin 13 mm machine guns. Note the brass strips between the joints of *Haguro*'s linoleum-covered deck. *Gakken*

POWs from the USS *Perch* (SS-176) on the deck of *Ushio*. The submarine had been damaged and then scuttled in the Java Sea on March 3, 1942. *Ushio* picked up the entire crew of fifty-nine, and they were brought to Balikpapan. *The Maru Special*

The destroyer *Ushio* refueling from the heavy cruiser *Haguro* at Kendari or Makassar, Celebes, perhaps on February 13, 1942. An oil hose can be seen next to the no. 1 torpedo mount. Note the large "mushroom"-shaped ventilators around the funnels, the 90 cm searchlight behind the second funnel, the loop antenna, and the twin 13 mm machine guns forward of the same funnel. The ship in this photo has also been identified as *Akebono* because on the forward funnel is painted the character *Ha* (は), indicating the 3rd ship in the division, which was *Akebono*. *The Maru Special*

Ushio at Saipan in April 1943. The photo was taken during the time when *Ushio* operated between Yokosuka and Truk, escorting escort carriers *Taiyō* and *Unyō*. *The Maru Special*

Ushio refuels from *Nippon Maru* at Truk in June 1943. As can be seen, the 12.7 cm gun mounts were partly revised during the ship's modification following the *Tomozuru* and 4th Fleet incidents. During high-speed runs, the cover of the aiming room could collapse if hit by waves, and this led to a remodeling of the cover, which became flat. Note the linoleum-covered deck and the checker plate beside the gun mount. *Gakken*

Hibiki off the Chinese coast, probably in 1937, after modification. Her bridge structure is substantially reduced in size, and the rounded edges of the forecastle deck are easy to see. Note the 3-meter rangefinder on top of the bridge structure. All destroyers of the third group had this larger type of rangefinder. *Naval Historical Center*

An aiming tower (*shōjuntō*) (also called a shooting tower [*shagekitō*]) that integrates a 3-meter rangefinder (*on top*) and a type 94 director (*hōiban shōjun sōchi*) on the upper bridge of *Hibiki*. At the far right is the commander's seat, with a 12 cm telescope. A windshield of a 66 cm rangefinder is shown in the foreground. *Gakken*

Inazuma at Yokosuka in 1934. The ship is at anchor, awnings are spread, portholes are open, and the accommodation ladder is lowered. The scene expresses a rather relaxed atmosphere. At that time there were twelve special-type destroyers belonging to the 6th, 7th, 8th, and 10th Destroyer Divisions at Yokosuka. The others were based at Kure. Note the 3-meter rangefinder on top of the large bridge structure.

Ushio underwent a modification at Yokosuka Navy Yard (*kōshō*) from September 4 to October 5, 1943, and her antiaircraft armament was augmented. The 13 mm machine guns forward of the bridge were replaced by a twin 25 mm mount. The 2-meter rangefinder between torpedo mounts no. 2 and 3 was replaced by two triple 25 mm mounts, and 12.7 cm main gun no. 2 was also replaced with two triple 25 mm mounts. The two 13 mm twin mounts forward of the second funnel were removed. Radar type 22 was installed on the foremast, and the 2-meter rangefinder on the bridge structure was replaced with a 3-meter type. Between May 25 and June 7, 1944 (or possibly in August–September), *Ushio*'s torpedo tubes were converted to be able to launch the type 93 oxygen torpedoes. This photo shows *Ushio* at Yokosuka in October 1943. *Kure Maritime Museum*

Close-up of the aftermost part of *Ushio* in May 1943, while she was operating in the central Pacific along the Yokosuka–Truk line. Crew members are training using a 12.7 cm loading-exercise machine. The rectangular box to the rear is a bulletproof plate for depth charges, and behind it are two smoke ejectors. To the left can be seen some depth charges. *Gakken*

CHAPTER 8

Complement

The planned complement was ten officers, three warrant officers, and 194 petty officers and ratings—a total of 207 officers and men. But the complement must have been increased as more weapons, for example, were fitted; however, the data are lacking.

On board *Sazanami* at Maizuru, May 19, 1932. The commissioning ceremony is underway on the quarter deck, and Shōsa (Commander) Inagaki Yoshiaki is taking command. The joints of the hull plates can be seen, and there is no doubt that they are welded. Also seen in this photo is the end of the depth-charge-dropping rails, the propeller guard, and a swinging boom. *Gakken*

Endnotes

CHAPTER 1

1. The torpedo boats of the Chidori and Ōtori classes.

2. For more details, see John Jordan, ed., *Warship 2013* (London: Conway, 2013), 41–42.

CHAPTER 2

1. Basic designs F 41D1 to F 41D3.

2. Later modified and refined.

3. In combination with this, the torpedo power of the Mutsuki class (1,315 tons, 38.5 knots), whose construction was to start in fiscal year 1924, was to be strengthened by mounting three twin 61 cm torpedo tubes. As a reason for the shift from 53 cm to 61 cm torpedo tubes, the Naval General Staff explained that the underwater protection of battleships and heavy cruisers had been reinforced considerably in the previous few years, so the explosive charge of the 53 cm type could not generate sufficient destructive power. Because the torpedo would form the main battle weapon of the destroyers in the future and because the 53 cm torpedo had no space to increase its explosive charge and improve its speed, the best measure was to equip future first-class destroyers with the 61 cm torpedo. This torpedo would provide improved destructive power (by a heavier explosive charge) and hitting probability (by higher speed) and, hence, fulfill the requirements resulting from improved protection and higher speed of the capital ship and its substitute (the heavy cruiser).

4. After referring to the postponement of the construction due to the 1923 Great Kantō earthquake, Adm. Yamashita pointed out the increase in the destroyer type in the French navy and expressed the fear that "the Royal Navy and the United States Navy will follow this trend in the foreseeable future. If the IJN adheres to the current ship type, most of the ready-built and planned destroyers will become outdated very quickly, even before they are sailing on the sea. The principle of the shipbuilding policy of the IJN is the superior power of the individual ship. This necessity is felt very strongly if the current forces and conditions are compared with those of the USN. Therefore, the supplementation program for the construction of thirty-six large destroyers is submitted. In view of the aforementioned situation, time is ripe to change some of the destroyers whose construction is already planned."

5. In a very long and interesting lecture titled "Outline of the design of warships of world navies" to the crown prince (later Emperor Hirohito) on December 18, 1924, Hiraga stated that other nations emphasize seaworthiness and endurance and prefer the construction of large-size destroyers. He pointed out that "IJN destroyers are good but should be improved in these respects in order to become more seaworthy and have longer endurance. To attain this goal, only first-class destroyers should be built."

CHAPTER 3

1. Readers interested in this incident may refer to Jordan, *Warship 2013*, 30–45, for an outline.

CHAPTER 4

1. This particular shape was very effective for improving seaworthiness and was afterward also adopted in the destroyers of the Hatsuharu class and in the torpedo boats of the Chidori class. However, the "tumble-home" method was abolished after the "Fourth Fleet incident" because of its negative effect on hull strength.

2. The flare resembled the shape of a Japanese vetch and is often compared to this flower by Japanese authors.

3. This material reacted with seawater, and after ten years, holes appeared. Hori Motoyoshi describes that he and his colleagues, who became naval architects at that time, considered a solution of this problem a big task. In the end, plates were sometimes replaced by pure aluminum.

4. Officers below the commanding officer were usually very young and seldom experienced.

5. Refer to Jordan, *Warship 2007*, 107, table 11, to see that in comparison to the Hatsuharu class, the improvement was truly only "a little bit."

CHAPTER 6

1. Mainly *Kaigun Kikanshi* ("History of naval machinery") (Tokyo: Hara Shobō, 1975), 2:692–701, with omissions.

2. Generally speaking, endurance depends mainly on the effective performance of the propulsion plant and the fuel storage. The performance of the machinery was improved, but the scale was rather low compared with the main and auxiliary machines designed a few years later. The designed fuel storage was 454 tons in order to attain 4,150 nm / 14 knots, but almost 500 tons was actually stored.

CHAPTER 7

1. It is sometimes said that the four ships of the *Akatsuki* group mounted only twelve torpedoes, but this seems to be very questionable.

2. However, from crews' evidence, the historian Tamura Toshio has stated (letter to Lars Ahlberg, September 12, 2001) that not all Fubuki-class destroyers received the type 93 torpedoes. According to Mr. Tamura, only six special-type destroyers were converted to launch the type 93s: *Hibiki* (Yokosuka, August 1943), *Yūgiri* (Kure, August–November 1943), *Usugumo* (Ōminato, June 1944), *Uranami* (September 1944), *Ushio* (August–September 1944), and *Akebono* (August–September 1944). He also specifically stated that although the following had the opportunity, while under repair, to be converted, they were not: *Shikinami*, *Sazanami*, *Shirakumo*, *Amagiri*, *Ikazuchi*, and *Inazuma*. According to *Toku Gata Kuchikukan* ("Special-type destroyers") (Tokyo: Gakken, 2010), *Ushio* was converted at Ōminato between 25 May and 7 June 1944.

3. Designed and planned to be mounted on cruisers, it was first fitted on light cruisers, but afterward it was changed to destroyers and was fitted mainly on this warship type.

4. The oxygen torpedo was classified as a top military secret, and the oxygen generator was ranked in the class below. Thus the use of the term "oxygen" was strictly prohibited, and even Nippon Sanso KK (Japan Oxygen Company) had to change the name to Nippon Rika (Science and Chemistry) Kōgyō KK in 1936 and had to establish a top-secret factory.

5. For aircraft carriers and cruisers as well as submarine tenders, the larger type 2 (type 93 and type 94 generators, respectively), with a capacity of 30 m^3/hour, was designed and manufactured.

6. This condition could not be obtained, since no attempt was made to maintain the column in a vertical position and, by this means, to render the oxygen production independent of the roll of the ship. When the angle was below 5°, the purity of the oxygen exceeded 98%. Larger angles (less than 10°) could be compensated for by reducing the output of oxygen to attain the necessary purity.

7. Before adoption, the column had been tested in three different positions (5°, 10°, and 15°) against the vertical to simulate listing and pitching of the ship, and the special shape and arrangement of the plates (a secret patent) had been chosen to obtain this result.

8. In addition, the power should be sufficient to enable a destroyer division, formed of two to four ships, to fight against an enemy light cruiser, with a good chance of victory.

9. More details can be found in Jordan, *Warship 2007*, 91–110, particularly on pp. 96–97.

10. The initial ammunition supply was 150/180 projectiles per gun in peacetime and wartime, respectively, but it was reduced to 120/150 after reconstruction.

11. It is said that two 6.6 mm machine guns, primarily for use by the naval landing force, were also mounted.